modern publicity

1975/76

modern publicity

1975/76

Editor Felix Gluck

A Studio Book

The Viking Press New York

Copyright © 1975 by Studio Vista. All rights reserved Published in 1975 in London by Studio Vista, a division of Cassell & Collier Macmillan Publishers Limited, London, 35 Red Lion Square, London WC1R 4SG, Sydney, Auckland, Toronto, Johannesburg, an affiliate of Macmillan Publishing Co. Inc., New York and in New York in 1976 by The Viking Press Inc., 625 Madison Avenue, New York, NY 10022.

British ISBN 0 289 70613 0.
United States SBN 670-48388-5.
Library of Congress Catalog card number: 26-17746.

Printed and bound in the Netherlands by
4P Drukkerij Reclame BV, Rotterdam.

Contents

Sommaire

Inhalt

Abbreviations
Abkürzungen

AD   Advertiser
Client
Auftraggeber

AG   Agent
Agence
Reklameberater

DIR   Art Director
Directeur Artistique
Künstlerischer Leiter

DES/AR   Designer/artist
Maquettiste/artiste
Grafiker/Künstler

PRO   Producer
Production
Produktion

PH   Photographer

ST   Studio
Atelier

The cover of this year's edition of *Modern Publicity* is based on a French poster for the International Wool Secretariat, which intrigued everyone who saw it. The concept was brilliant and the team who solved the problem of finding the right location, the right shepherd and the right photographic solution to produce the final subtle effect, provided a supreme example of co-ordination.

The sheep posters on page 24 were produced by an English team. Again ingenious co-ordination (the sheep were actually shampooed before being photographed) and the brilliant idea of showing nothing but a four-legged wool factory produced delightful results. The clients, the International Wool Secretariat, have obviously managed to achieve equally high standards of ideas and presentation in all their national operations without imposing any central formulas. The Italian Carabinieri hat (p. 72–73), the humour of the German or Japanese advertisements and the difference of approach between the French and English fashion advertisements all show distinct national solutions.

Letraset International too leaves design freedom to its international subsidiaries, but here some successful German publicity may appear in English or Scandinavian prospectuses. The material advertised by Letraset, of course, adds a certain unity whereever and in whatever form it is shown. It will be interesting if our contributors send in more international advertising campaigns to enable our readers to analyse more approaches.

In our poster section I would like to comment on the Peugeot campaign by Delpire Advico who used Seymour Chwast, Bernard Durin and Milton Glaser to convey an atmosphere of humorous nostalgia in their posters.

In the Press Advertisement section we have used the Dutch Milk Marketing Board advertisements to open the section. Their painted cows have an absurd surrealist quality which cannot fail to attract the attention of the public.

The type specimen book by Berthold has the functionalism and precision of a high-quality instrument and is a pleasure to handle.

As promised in the last edition, we have introduced a new section on postage stamp designs. Our opening pages show stamps illustrating three different subjects used by various countries. As this was the first time we asked for entries for this chapter, our choice was still limited and we kept the section to six pages only. I do hope that in the future we will have more entries from designers and postal directorates to illustrate more graphic and new technical solutions in stamp design and printing.

We introduce the packaging chapter with Olaf Leu's superb sample box of folded cartons which was sent out by Zanders-Ikonolux for publicity. It shows the paper to its best advantage and also provides a real service to designers in its variety of ideas for folding as well as in the packaging encyclopaedia supplied with this box. The presentation of the whole box is an additional delight.

In the Trademark Section we are showing a series of signpostings for a children's hospital in Buenos Aires, designed by Guillermo Gonzalez Ruiz. It is a concept of brilliant simplicity and humour which could be used anywhere in the world.

For the opener of the Direct Mail section, we have used the paper publicity campaigns by Robert Burns. Bond paper which is one of those advertised, is a paper which has traditionally been used for bonds and shares. The designers have used this as a basis for a set of humorous texts advertising fictitious companies.

Once again, I would like to thank all the designers, agencies, teams and clients from all over the world, who have contributed their work for this annual. I hope they will send in their new entries again and that those designers whose work we did not manage to include this year will not be discouraged from entering their work for the next volume.

La couverture de l'édition de *Modern Publicity* de cette année est basée sur l'affiche qui intrigua tout le monde qui la vit. Ce fut une brillante idée et l'équipe qui résolut le problème de trouver la location idéale, le berger idéal et la meilleure solution photographique pour produire l'effet final astucieux, donne un merveilleux exemple de coordination.

Les affiches des moutons montrées à la page 24, ont été produites par une équipe anglaise. A nouveau, une coordination ingénieuse (les moutons eurent à subir un schampooing avant d'être photographiés) et l'idée astucieuse de montrer uniquement une usine à laine à quatre pattes, donnèrent des résultats charmants. Il est évident que les clients, le Secrétariat International de la Laine, ont réussi à garder une très grande qualité de présentation et d'idées dans toutes leurs opérations nationales, sans pour autant vouloir imposer un thème sur un sujet central. Le chapeau du carabinier italien (page 72), l'humour de la réclame allemande ou japonaise, ou bien encore la façon différente d'aborder le sujet de la publicité de mode, des français ou des anglais, tout cela montre les approches bien distinctes des différents pays.

Letraset International laisse aussi la liberté d'expression à ses auxiliaires internationaux, mais ici par exemple, quelques-unes des publicités allemandes les plus réussies paraîtront dans des catalogues anglais ou suédois. Bien sûr le matériel dont Letraset fait la réclame offre une certaine unité quelque soit la façon ou l'endroit où il est représenté. Cela serait intéressant que nos collaborateurs envoient plus de campagnes publicitaires de tous pays afin de permettre à nos lecteurs d'analyser différentes approches.

Dans notre chapitre sur les affiches, j'aimerais parler de la campagne Peugeot par Delpire-Advico qui a utilisé Seymour Chwast, Bernard Durin et Milton Glaser pour rendre à leurs affiches une atmosphère nostalgique pleine d'humour.

Nous avons utilisé la réclame du Comité Laitier Hollandais pour ouvrir le chapitre de la publicité dans la presse. Leurs vaches peintes ont une qualité surréaliste et absurde qui ne manquera pas d'attirer l'attention du public.

Le catalogue de caractères d'imprimerie de Berthold est d'une clarté et d'une précision qui en font un instrument de travail de grande qualité qui est un plaisir à utiliser.

Ainsi que promis dans notre dernier volume, nous avons ouvert un nouveau chapitre sur les projets de timbres-poste. Nos pages d'introduction présentent des timbres illustrant trois sujets différents utilisés par divers pays. Notre choix est encore limité du fait que c'est la première fois que nous demandons du matériel pour cette section; nous n'y avons donc consacré que six pages. J'espère que dorénavant les artistes et la direction des postes nous enverront beaucoup de sujets pour notre prochaîne sélection . . .

En introduction au chapitre de l'emballage, nous montrons une magnifique boîte échantillon faite de carton plié, envoyée comme publicité par les papiers Zanders-Ikonolux. Cela montre le papier à son plus grand avantage et rend aussi un réel service aux dessinateurs par l'abondance des façons de pliages et par une 'encyclopédie de l'emballage' remise avec cette boîte. La présentation de la boîte entière est à elle seule un plaisir.

Dans le chapitre des marques de fabriques, nous montrons une série de signes pour un hôpital pour enfants, une idée originale dessinée par Guillermo Gonzalez Ruiz, simple et pleine d'humour qui pourrait être utilisée dans le monde entier.

Pour l'introduction du chapitre sur les brochures, nous avons utilisé les campagnes publicitaires pour le papier de Robert Burns. Le papier Bond, qui est l'une des marques en réclame, est un papier sur lequel furent traditionnellement imprimés titres et valeurs. Les dessinateurs ont utilisé ceci comme base pour une série de textes humoristiques vantant des sociétés imaginaires.

Une fois de plus, j'aimerais remercier dessinateurs, agences, équipes et clients du monde entier, dont les travaux ont contribué à la création de ce volume. J'espère que tous enverront bientôt de nouveaux sujets et que les dessinateurs dont nous n'avons pas eu la possibilité de montrer les œuvres, ne se décourageront pas d'inscrire celles-ci pour notre prochain volume.

Die Umschlagsillustration für unsere diesjährige Ausgabe basiert auf einem französischem Plakat für das Internationale Wollsekretariat, das alle Passanten verwundert haben muss. Die Konzeption war brilliant und das Team hat die Ko-ordinationsprobleme, die richtige Lokalität zu finden, den geeigneten Schäfer und Schafe bereit zu haben und auch die vollkommene photographische Komposition zu erreichen, durch hervorragende Zusammenarbeit gelöst.

Die Schafplakate auf Seite 24 wurden von einem englischen Team entworfen. Wiederum war es die erfinderische Ko-ordination (die Schafe wurden sogar schampuniert bevor sie photographiert wurden) und die Idee, nichts anderes als eine vierbeinige Wollfabrik mit gutem Text zu zeigen, die zu dem Resultat eines Riesenerfolges in England führten.

Dem Kunden, dem Internationalen Wollsekretariat, ist es klar gelungen, einen gleich hohen Standard von Ideen und Präsentationen in allen nationalen Operationen zu erreichen ohne auf zentrale Formeln zu bestehen.

Auf Seite 72 sehen wir andere Beispiele der Wollwerbung. Den italienischen Carabinerihut, den Humor der deutschen und japanischen Inserate zusammen mit der unterschiedlichen Behandlung des französischen und englischen Modemarktes.

Letraset International überlasst die Entwurfsfreiheit auch den nationalen Branchen. Hier kann es aber oft vorkommen, dass ein erfolgreicher deutscher Entwurf z.B. in englischen oder skandinavischen Prospekten wieder erscheint. Obwohl die Kataloge einen gemeinsamen Hausstil haben, kann man doch einen ziemlichen Unterschied im Lay-out der verschiedenen Gruppen finden (Seiten 86—87). Das Letraset-Material hat allerdings eine gewisse Einheit an sich. Wir hoffen aber, dass unsere Einsender in den nächsten Ausgaben noch mehr internationale Kampagnen senden um unseren Lesern die Möglichkeit zu weiteren Vergleichen zu geben.

In unserem Plakatkapitel möchte ich die Peugeot-Kampagne der Delpire-Advico Agentur besonders hervorheben. Seymour Chwast, Bernard Durin und Milton Glaser haben eine Atmosphere humorvoller Nostalgie geschaffen.

Für die Öffnungsseiten der Inserate haben wir die Kampagne der Holländischen Milchzentrale gewählt. Die bemalten Kühe haben eine absurde surrealistische Qualität, die unzweifelhaft die Aufmerksamkeit des Publikums erreichen wird.

Das Berthold Schrift-Musterbuch hat den Funktionalismus und die durchgedachte Präzision eines feinmechanischen Instruments. Es ist eine Freude damit zu arbeiten.

Wie wir in unsere letzten Ausgabe ankündigten, haben wir ein neues Kapitel für Briefmarkengrafik eingefügt. Unsere Öffnungsseiten illustrieren Marken die von verschiedenen Nationen zum selben Thema herausgegeben wurden. Da wir dieses Jahr zum ersten Mal Material für dieses Kapitel verlangten, war unsere Auswahlmöglichkeit noch ziemlich beschränkt. Wir haben darum nur sechs Seiten für dieses Kapitel verwendet. Ich hoffe aber, dass wir in der Zukunft mehr Material von Entwerfern und Postdirektionen erhalten werden. Die Briefmarkengrafik wird von vielen unserer Teilnehmer bearbeitet. Je mehr wir zur Auswahl bekommen, desto besser können wir interessante grafische und technische Lösungen illustrieren.

Das Verpackungskapitel wird dieses Jahr durch Olaf Leus superben Musterwürfel von Faltschachteln eingeleitet. Zanders-Ikonolux zeigt hier einige Anwendungsmöglichkeiten und deren Ausführung. Das kleine Lexikon, das dem Würfel beigelegt war (wiederum in einer geeigneten Faltschachtel) dient dem Grafiker mit weiteren Ratschlägen. Die Präsentation und Wellkartonverpackung der Sendung gibt uns noch extra Genuss.

Auf der Öffnungsseite der Warenzeichen-sektion illustrieren wir mit einer Serie von Symbolen für ein Kinderkrankenhaus in Buenos Aires, die von Guillermo Gonzalez Ruiz entworfen wurden. Es ist ein Konzept von humorvoller Simplizität, das überall in der Welt verwendet werden sollte.

Das Kapitel für Broschüren und Jahresberichte wurde durch eine Papierkampagne von Robert Burns eingeleitet. Bond-papier, das hier angeboten wird, wurde traditionell für Wertpapiere und Aktien verwendet. Das Team hat dies als Basis für eine Serie von humorvollen Beschreibungen von Phantasie-firmen verwendet.

Wie immer, danke ich allen Grafikern, Werbeagenturen, Teams und Firmen aus der ganzen Welt, die mit ihren Einsendungen zum Interesse und zu der Vielfältigkeit dieses Buches beigetragen haben und ich hoffe, dass auch jene wiederum Material einsenden werden, deren Arbeiten wir dieses Jahr nicht zeigen konnten.

Felix Gluck

INDEX

Artists, designers photographers, producers and art directors

Maquettistes et artistes, photographes, production et directeurs artistiques

Entwerfer, Photographen, Produktion und künstlerische Leiter

Clients

Posters
Affiches
Plakate

1a-b

1c

1a-e France
AD Peugeot
AG Delpire Advico
DIR Yosiane Chauderon
ILL Seymour Chwast (c, e)
    Bernard Durin (a)
    Milton Glaser (b, d)

1d -e

1

2

4

5

3

1 Austria
AD Litega
AG Graphik Studio Hauch
DIR/DES Walter J. Hauch
Summer sales, Soldes d'été, Sommer-
Inventur-Verkauf

2 Spain
AD Real Club de Tenis Barcelona
DES Enric Huguet
75th anniversary of tennis club,
75ème anniversaire d'un club de tennis,
75. Geburtstag eines Tennisklubs

3 Great Britain
AD London Transport Executive
AG London Transport Publicity
DIR A. B. Beaumont
DES David Gentleman
London transport

4 Switzerland
AD Festival de Musique
Montreux-Vevey
AG Publicité Bornand & Gaeng
DIR/ILL Bruno Gaeng
Concert series

5 Germany
AD Stadt Aachen
DES Klaus Endrikat
PHOTO Anne Gold
Artists of Aachen in Rheims, Artistes
d'Aix la Chapelle à Rheims, Aachener
Künstler in Rheims

6 United States
AD Student Services West
AG Gauger Sparks Silva
DIR/DES/COPY David Gauger
ILL David Gauger, Randy Lamorte
Travel

6

1a-c Germany
AD Wega Radio GmbH
AG Leonhardt & Kern
DIR/DES Hans Peter Kamm
ILL Ernst Wirz
Television and Hi-Fi equipment

2 Norway
AD Den Norske Bokklubben
DES Hansjørgen Toming
Bookclub promotion

3 United States
AD Adco Inc.
AG Stevensessions Design
DIR/DES Steven Sessions
COPY George James
Film animation

4 Iran
AD Institute for Intellectual Development
of Children and Young Adults
DES Farshid Mesghali
Anniversary of Institute

1a

3

Der feinste Ton klingt rein - mit Wega hifi.

1b

Eine Tuba klingt wie eine Tuba mit Wega HiFi.

1c

2

4

1 Germany
AD Neue Filmkunst, Walter Kirchner
DES Hans Hillmann
Film

2a-b Great Britain
AD Times Publishing Co.
AG Leo Burnett Ltd.
DIR Ken Mullen, Bob Byrne, Mike Brant
Newspaper, Journal, Zeitung

3 Finland
AD Seepra: Noutaa
AG Varis Poteri Veistola Oy
ILL Kyösti Varis
Printing, Imprimerie, Druckerei

4 United States
AD Penn. State University
AG Lanny Sommese Free Lance Design
DES Lanny Sommese
Art Exhibition

5 Finland
AD/AG Weilin & Göös
DIR/DES Olof Stenius
Book poster, Affiche pour un livre,
Buchplakat

6 United States
AD Little People's School
DES Joe Landry
School for deaf children, Ecole pour
enfants sourds, Schule für taube Kinder

7 Great Britain
AD The Other Cinema
DES Oscar Zarate
Film

1

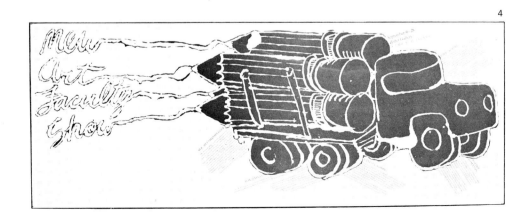

4

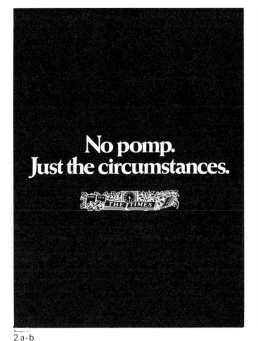

**No pomp.
Just the circumstances.**

**Sit down
with a paper of standing.**

2 a-b

SEEPRA≡NOUTAA

Kiviranta Graafinen laitos 88 11 66

3

PETER
BENCHLEY **TAPPAJA HAI** **SYKSYN
KIRJASENSAATIO**

WEILIN·GÖÖS

5

6

7

Little
People's
School

hope for deaf and
speech impaired
children

1507 Washington St.
W. Newton, Mass.
02165

HAPPINESS
Distributed by The Other Cinema

a film by Alexander Medvedkin
USSR 1934   'Today I saw how a bolshevik laughs'. Sergei Eisenstein

Graphic Design: Oscar Zarate

(cacharel)

1

4a 4b

Fashion in pure new wool.
By courtesy of Louise.

Pure new wool. There is nothing like it.

Winter in style this year, in a pure
wool coat.
Very chic Annabelle.

Pure new wool. There is nothing like it.

2

3

1 France
AD Cacharel
AG Delpire Advico
DIR Robert Delpire
DES Robert Sadoux
PHOTO Sarah Moon
Fashion

2 Finland
AD Volkswagen
AG Varis Poteri Veistola Oy
ILL Kyösti Varis
Automobiles

3 Switzerland
AD Amag AG
AG Hans Looser
DIR Matthias Blatter
DES Robert Hotl
PHOTO Nicolas Bossard
Automobiles

4a-b Great Britain
AD International Wool Secretariat
AG Davidson, Pearce, Berry &
Spottiswoode
DIR/DES Brian Bridge
PHOTO Adrian Flowers
COPY Phillip Gough
Wool-marketing

5 Germany
AD Stadt Nürnberg
DES Michael Mathías Prechtl
Lithographic work

6 Finland
AD Tampella
AG Varis Poteri Veistola Oy
PHOTO Kaj G. Lindholm
Fashion fabric

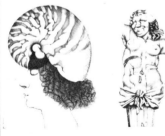

5

6

1

2

3

6

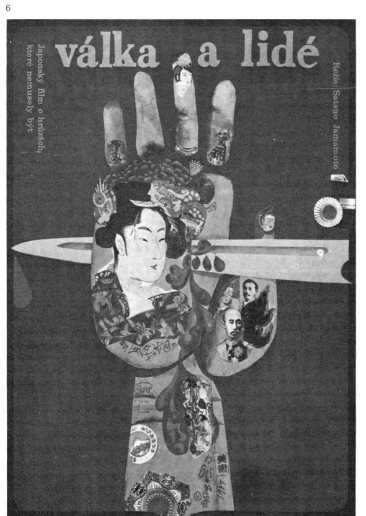

7

4

5

8a-b

Cool. Crisp. Dutch. Tomatoes.

Take one lettuce and separate the leaves.
Slice or chop one green and one red pepper.
Thinly slice one Golden Delicious apple
and half a cucumber. Slice four tomatoes.
Add 50 grammes (2 ounces) of walnuts and
mix well.
Serve as a side dish in four separate bowls.
Then add the special Yoghourt dressing,
made with natural Yoghourt with added salt,
pepper and a little garlic.
Include a little tomato juice to taste and mix
thoroughly.

Cool. Crisp. Delft Salad.

1a   1b

Bournville.
Whenever you've got the odd tomatoes.

4a

Bournville.
Whenever you've got the odd moment.

4b

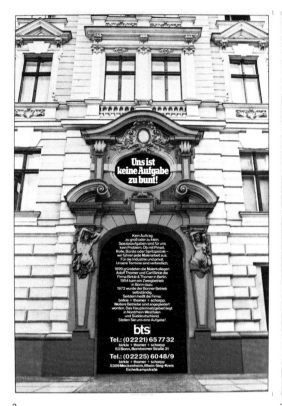

2

3

1a-b Great Britain
AD Dutch Fruit and Vegetable Bureau
AG Roe Humphreys Ltd
DIR/DES Paul Arden
PHOTO David Thorpe
Fruit and vegetables, Fruits et légumes,
Früchte und Gemüse

2 Germany
AD Birkle & Thomer & Schorpp
AG Atelier Noth & Hauer
DES Volker Noth, Cordes Hauer, Peter
Soderman
Housepainters, Peintres en bâtiments,
Malereibetrieb

3 Germany
AD Verkehrsamt Berlin
DES Jürgen Spohn
Tourism

4a-b Great Britain
AD Cadbury Bros Ltd.
AG Leo Burnett Ltd.
DIR Ken Mullen, Bob Byrne
Chocolate

5 France
AD Evry Town Council
AG Delpire Advico
DES/ILL André François
Tourism

5

Evry 1, ville à voir, ville à vivre.

Centre d'information sur place

wie wir leben wie wir leben

1a-b

ARIEL DORFMAN
'CULTURAL REPRESSION IN CHILE'
Symposium on Latin American Culture
15 Oct 8pm

Royal College of Art Kensington Gore SW7

2

5

History has shown that the birth rate only falls significantly when the
standard of living rises significantly for the majority of the people

World Population Year

Population

Gross National Product

First World   Second World   Third World

6

"O controle da poluição do ar e das águas
não deve ser decorrência de imposição legal
mas sim um imperativo da consciência individual"

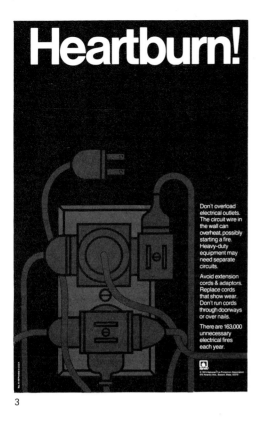

3

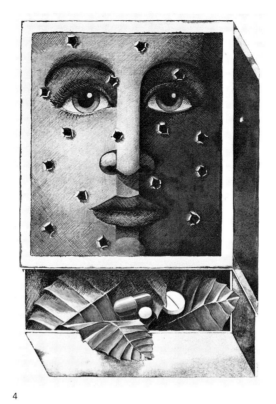

4

7a-b

British Painting '74 Hayward Gallery
Arts Council of Great Britain 26 September to 17 November 1974
Monday to Friday 10 to 8 / Saturdays 10 to 6 / Sundays 12 to 6
Admission 30p / Children, students and pensioners 15p
10p all day Monday and between 6 to 8 Tuesdays to Fridays

1

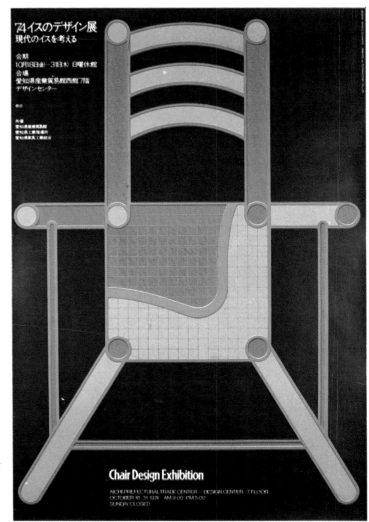

Chair Design Exhibition

AICHI PREFECTURAL TRADE CENTER - DESIGN CENTER - 7 FLOOR
OCTOBER 18 - 31 1974 - AM 9:00 - PM 5:00
SUNDAY CLOSED

2

たのしい語らい ——— FAMILY CHRISTMAS シキシマパン

4

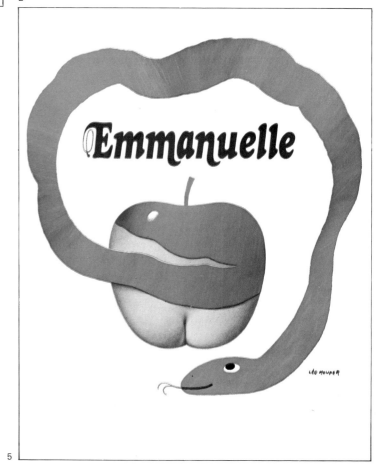

5

PEACOCK-INDIAN NATIONAL BIRD
AIR-INDIA

1 Great Britain
AD Arts Council
AG Pentagram Design Partnership
DIR/DES Alan Fletcher
Exhibition of British painting

2 Japan
AD Aichi Trade Center
DIR/DES Shigeo Okamoto
Exhibition

3 India
AD Air India
AG Air India Art Studio
DIR J. B. Cowasji
DES Hans Erni
India

4 Japan
AD Shikishima Baking Co. Ltd.
DIR/DES Shigeo Okamoto
ILL Toshiyuki Ohashi
Christmas

5 France
AD Para Francefilm
DES Léo Kouper
Film

3

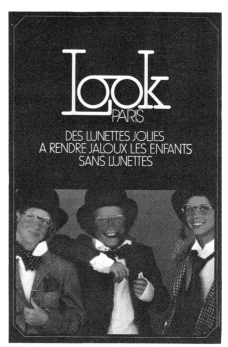

1a-c

3

4

AHORRE LA MITAD.
BANCA CATALANA PONE EL RESTO

2

5

LOTTUSSE. MODA EN PIEL

6

That's close enough.
Now smile.

KONICA

1a-c France
AD Look Paris
AG Delpire Advico
DIR Robert Delpire
DES Michel Cazell
PHOTO Sarah Moon
Spectacles, Lunettes, Brillen

2 Spain
AD Banca Catalana
AG Consejeros de Publicidad S.A.
DIR/DES Luis Duran
ILL A. Marly
COPY Felix Garate
Bank publicity, Publicité d'une banque,
Bankreklame

3 Great Britain
AD Observer Jewellery Competition
sponsored by the Welsh Arts Council
AG Design Systems
PHOTO Peter Jones
Jewellery exhibition, Exposition de
bijoux, Schmuckausstellung

4 France
AD André France
AG Mafia (Maimé Arnodin, Fayolle,
International Associés)
Shoes, Chaussures, Schuhe

5 Spain
AD Lorenzo Fuuxá
AG Consejeros de Publicidad S.A.
DIR/DES Alfonso Martin
ILL M. Martinez

6 Canada
AD Garlick Films Ltd.
AG Raymond Lee & Associates Ltd.
DIR/DES Raymond Lee
ILL Viktor von Madespach
COPY John Dymun
Cameras

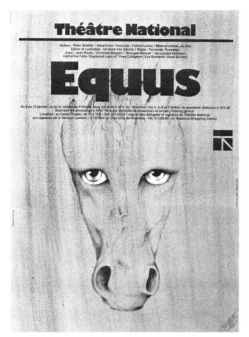

1a-b

2

4

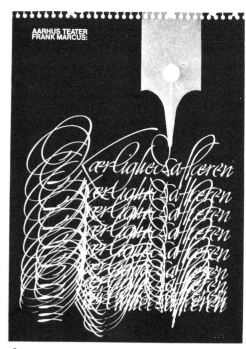

5

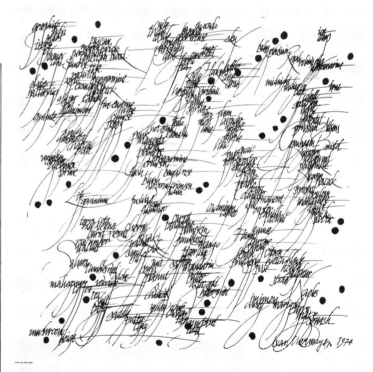

COLOR

an exhibition of original work

of distinguished artists, designers and photographers

from the United States and abroad

sponsored by

The American Institute of Graphic Arts

1974

the absolute sound

volume1 number4
spring 1974

3a-b

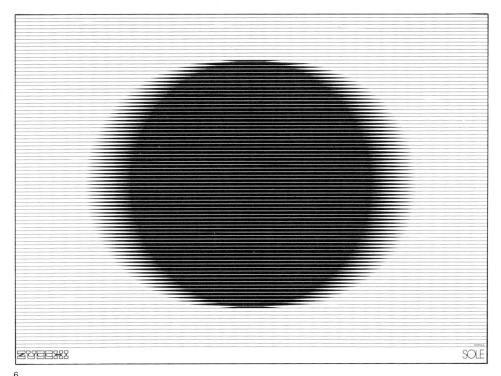

6

7

Exhibitions at
19 Charlotte Sq

Scottish
Arts Council
Gallery

Admission Free
Weekdays 10-6
Sundays 2-6
Coffee House

1a-b Belgium
AD Théâtre National
DES Manfred Hürig (a)
Manfred Hürig, Anna Velghe (b)
Theatre

2 Denmark
AS Aarhus Theatre
AG Finn Hjernöe's Grafiske Tegnestue
DIR/DES Finn Hjernöe
Theatre

3a-b United States
AD The Absolute Sound
AG G. Viskupic Design
DIR/DES Gary Viskupic
COPY Harry Pearson
Magazine for audiophiles, Revue Hi-Fi
spécialisée, Hi-Fi Magazin

4 United States
AD Material Research Laboratory
AG Lanny Sommese Free Lance Design
DIR/DES Lanny Sommese
Art show containing works which relate
to science, Exposition d'œuvres d'art
ayant un rapport avec la science,
Kunst und Wissenschaft-Ausstellung

5 United States
AD American Institute of Graphic Arts
AG Chermayeff & Geismar Associates
DIR/DES Ivan Chermayeff
Colour exhibition of original work,
Exposition en couleur de dessins
originaux

6 Italy
AD Telerie Zucchi S.p.A.
AG Studio Coppola
DIR/DES Silvio Coppola
Promotional posters, Affiches de
promotion

7 Great Britain
AD Scottish Arts Council
AG James Gardiner Associates
DIR James Gardiner
DES Pauline Gardiner
Scottish Arts Council exhibitions,
Expositions du conseil municipal de l'art
écossais

1 Mexico
AD Centro de Estudios Historicos del
Movimiento Obrero Mexicano
AG Gleason Diseño
DES Jorge Gleason
Center for historical studies, Centre
d'études historiques, Zentrum für
Geschichtsforschung

2 Spain
AD Renta Catalana
DES Pedro Ariño
Christmas campaign for bank,
Campagne de Noël d'une banque,
Weihnachtskampagne für eine Bank

3 Spain
AD IP Mark
AG Carlos Rolando & Asociados
DIR/DES Carlos Rolando
Seminar on advertising, Séminaire sur
la publicité, Reklameseminar

4 Germany
AD Kurpfälz, Kammerorchester
DES Wolf Magin
Concert

5 Germany
AD Staatstheater Darmstadt
AG Frieder Grindler Graphic Design
Ballet

6 Japan
AD Paruco
DIR Ikko Tanaka
DES Ikko Tanaka
PHOTO Haruo Takino
Poster gallery opening, Inauguration
d'une exposition d'affiches

7 Germany
AD Braunschweigisches Landesmuseum
AG Staatliche Hochschule für Bildende
Künste Braunschweig
DIR Prof. Klaus Grözinger
DES Herbert Tarrey
Farmhouse museum, Musée de la
ferme, Bauernhausmuseum

8 Germany
AD Tribüne Berlin
DES Peter Klemke
Theatre

9 United States
AD Art Department Penn. State
University
AG Lanny Sommese Free Lance Design
DES Lanny Sommese
ILL Joe Cancilla
Retrospective exhibition of Surrealist
art, Exposition rétrospective de l'art
surréaliste

4

5

6

8

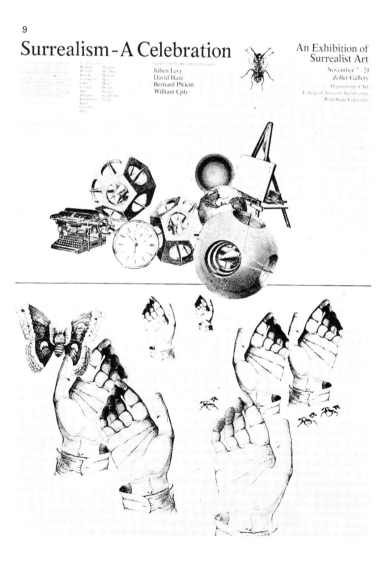

9

1

DAVID BULL Represented By CHRIS MEIKLEJOHN, 50-54 Beak Street London, W1. Tel: 01-734 5237

2

4

5

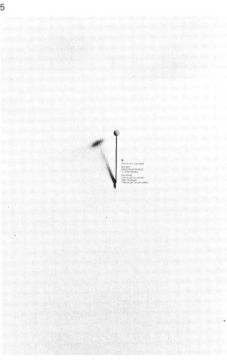

6

3

7

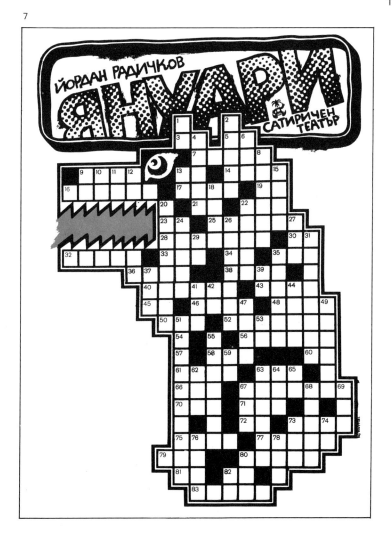

1a-b

2

4

5

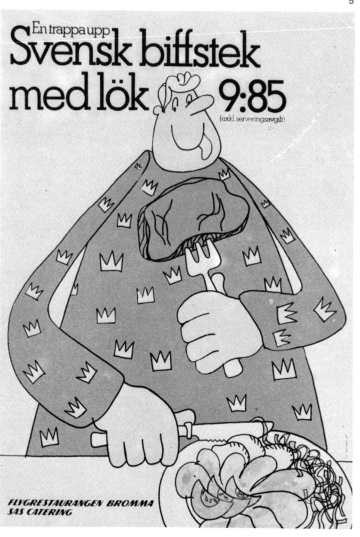

Mary Brown has the best legs in town.

Mary Brown's Fried Chicken ©

3

6

LA CAMPAGNA SI PRESENTA
CANCELLI APERTI

1a-b Holland
AD Het Nederlands Zuivelbureau
AG Prad B.V.
DIR Paul Mertz
TYPE DIR Gerard Unger
ILL Mariet Numan
COPY Paul Mertz
Invitation for children to come to the
demonstration kitchen, Invitation pour
enfants pour une démonstration
culinaire, Einladung für Kinder, zur
Demonstrationsküche zu kommen

2 Finland
AD Keskusosuusliike OTK
AG Mainosrengas Oy
DIR Pekka Vaara
DES Markku Asunta
ILL Kaj Ewart
COPY Mirja Öhman

3 Canada
AD Mary Brown Canada Ltd.
AG Raymond Lee & Associates Ltd.
DIR/DES Raymond Lee
ILL Christl-Sliva Photographers
Fried chicken, Poulet sauté, Brathuhn

4 Finland
AD Yhtyneet Paperitehtaat Oy,
Paperituote (United Paper Mills Ltd.)
AG Paperituote Advertising
DIR/DES Heikki Toivola
Polystyrene fish boxes, Emballage pour
poisson en polystyrene, Polystyrene
Schachteln, zum Verpacken von Fisch

5 Sweden
AD SAS Catering
AG Jim Åkerstedt AB
DIR/DES Jim Åkerstedt
Airport restaurant, Restaurant
d'aéroport, Flughafenrestaurant

6 Italy
AD Confederazione Generale
dell'Agricultura Italiana
AG Promos srl.
DIR Bob Elliott
DES/ILL John Alcorn
COPY Pia de Fazio
Italian agriculture, Agriculture en Italie,
Italienische Landwirtschaft

1 Italy
AD I.A.P. Industriale
AG Promos srl.
DIR/DES Bob Elliott
ILL Mario Zapallá
Honda motorcycle, Motocyclette Honda,
Motorräder

2a-b Italy
AD Ing. C. Olivetti & C., S.p.A.
AG DRCDIP/SPP
DIR/DES Ines Campagnoli (a),
Fulvio Ronchi, Ines Campagnoli (b)
PHOTO Alfredo Crabb (a)
ILL Ines Campagnoli (b)
COPY Giovanni Giudici (b)
Electronic Typewriters, Machines à
écrire électroniques

3 Sweden
AD Föreningen för arbetarskydd
AG Jim Åkerstedt AB
DIR/DES Jim Åkerstedt
ILL Svante Fischerström
Information about eye protection for
people in factories and offices,
Information pour la protection des yeux
dans les usines et les bureaux,
Unfallsverhütung

4 Germany
AD Deutsches Rundfunk-Museum
AG Atelier Noth & Hauer
DES Volker Noth, Cordes Hauer, Peter
Sodemann
Radio museum, Musée de la radio,
Rundfunkmuseum Berlin

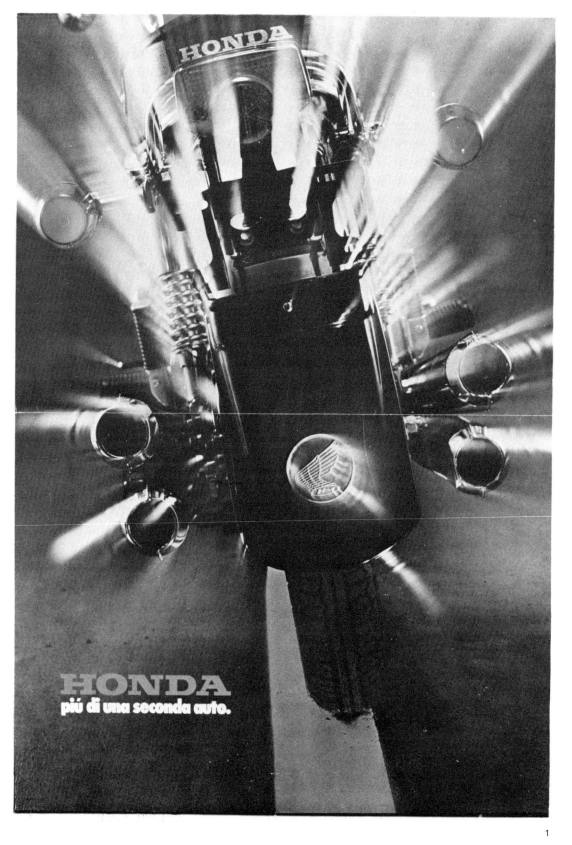

1

A 7

olivetti

Olivetti Studio 46

olivetti

2a 2b

BRA BELYSNING
Allmänbelysning·Platsbelysning·Planmässigt underhåll

Vilken belysning Du skall ha beror bl a på Din ålder och typ av arbete.
Är Du osäker, säg till vid nästa skyddsrond.

4

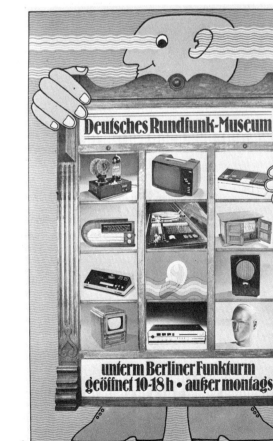

Deutsches Rundfunk-Museum

unterm Berliner Funkturm
geöffnet 10-18 h · außer montags

3

1

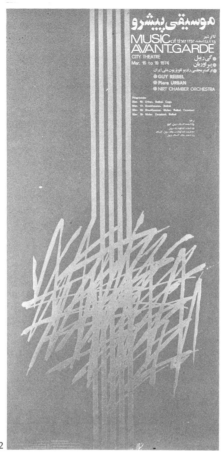

2

3

5

6

The Concert For Bangladesh

4

1 Switzerland
AD Opernhaus Zürich
AG MB & Co
DIR Ruedi Rüegg
DES Pete Spalinger
Opera

2 Iran
AD City Theatre
AG NIRT Graphic Dept., National Iranian
Radio & TV
DIR/DES Ghobad Shiva
Avant-garde music performance

3 Spain
AD Federación Catalana de Gimnasia
DES Pedro Ariño
Men's gymnastic event, Epreuve de
gymnastique pour hommes, Sportsfest

4 Norway
AD UNICEF
ILL Hansjørgen Toming
Concert for Bangladesh

5 Germany
AD Hans Christian Andersen Theater Kiel
DES Holger Matthies
Theatre

6 Germany
AD Kunst und Gewerbe Hamburg
DES Holger Matthies
Glass exhibition, Exposition de verrerie

7 Yugoslavia
AD Belgrade International Theatre
Festival
AG Studio Structure
DIR/DES Slobodan Masic
Theatre festival

7

filmska parada

5 međunarodni festival filmova za decu i omladinu 28. januar - 6. februar 1975.

dom pionira beograda

dom pionira i omladine voždovac
bioskop šumadija čukarica
dom kulture vuk karadžić
dom ratnog vazduhoplovstva zemun
radnički univerzitet novi beograd

1

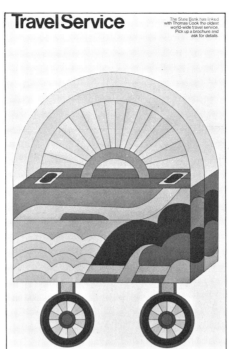

Travel Service

The State Bank has linked
with Thomas Cook the oldest
world-wide travel service.
Pick up a brochure and
ask for details.

2

3

5

Was soll ich schenken?
Was soll ich mir wünschen?
Die Werkbücherei zeigt vom
11. Dezember 1972 bis
6. Januar 1973 in ihren
Räumen eine Auswahl der
1972 erschienenen Bücher

Öffnungszeiten:
Montag – Freitag von
10.00 Uhr bis 13.30 Uhr und
von 15.00 Uhr bis 19.00 Uhr
Samstag von 9.00 Uhr
bis 14.00 Uhr, Katalog
wird kostenlos abgegeben

Weihnachten mit Büchern

6

WON'T IT BE NICE...
WHEN ALL THE WORLD'S SOLDIERS
ARE PARADING ONLY
UNDER CHRISTMAS TREES.

WE WISH YOU PEACE!

BOB, CARMEN, BRENT & BRIAN COONTS

4

7

1 United States
AD NBC Television Network
AG NBC Television Network Marketing
Dept.
DES Bob Greenwell
PHOTO Dan Baliotti
Hockey

2 Japan
AD Japan Pottery Design Center
DIR/DES Shigeo Okamoto
ILL Toshiyuki Ohashi
Pottery design competition, Concours
pour la meilleure poterie

3 Germany
AD Bayerischer Rundfunk
DES Walter Tafelmaier
ILL Michael Tafelmaier
Concert series, Série de concerts

4 Germany
AD Senator für Arbeit & Soziales
AG Atelier Noth & Hauer
DES Volker Noth, Cordes Hauer, Peter
Sodemann
Old people's entertainment programmes,
Programmes de divertissements pour
personnes agées, Veranstaltungen für
Senioren

1

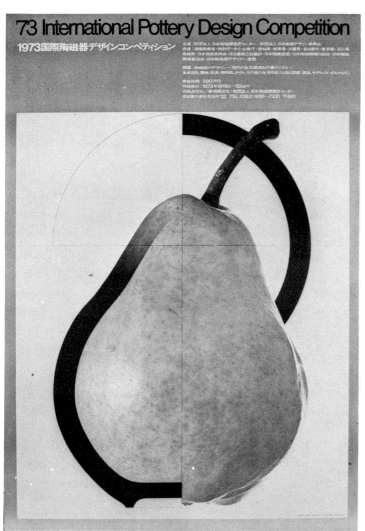

73 International Pottery Design Competition

1973国際陶磁器デザインコンペティション

2

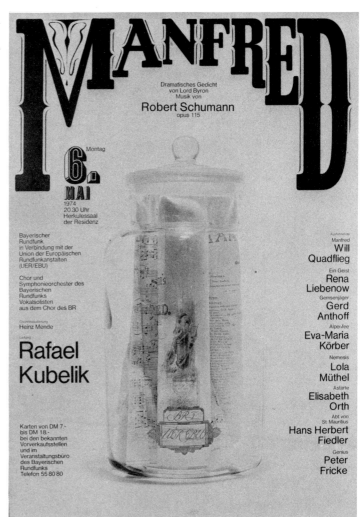

MANFRED

Dramatisches Gedicht
von Lord Byron
Musik von
Robert Schumann
opus 115

6. Montag
MAI
1974
20.30 Uhr
Herkulessaal
der Residenz

Bayerischer
Rundfunk
in Verbindung mit der
Union der Europäischen
Rundfunkanstalten
(UER/EBU)

Chor und
Symphonieorchester des
Bayerischen
Rundfunks
Vokalsolisten
aus dem Chor des BR

Choreinstudierung:
Heinz Mende

Leitung:
**Rafael
Kubelik**

Karten von DM 7,-
bis DM 18,-
bei den bekannten
Vorverkaufsstellen
und im
Veranstaltungsbüro
des Bayerischen
Rundfunks
Telefon 55 80 80

Ausführende
Manfred
**Will
Quadflieg**

Ein Geist
**Rena
Liebenow**

Gemsenjäger
**Gerd
Anthoff**

Alpenfee
**Eva-Maria
Körber**

Nemesis
**Lola
Müthel**

Astarte
**Elisabeth
Orth**

Abt von
St. Mauritius
**Hans Herbert
Fiedler**

Genius
**Peter
Fricke**

3

4

1 Holland
AD Poppentheater 'Guido van Deth'
DES Ralph Prins
Puppet theatre

2 Great Britain
AD Anthony Chardet Productions Ltd.
AG Friends Design Workshop Ltd.
DIR/DES Clifford Richards
A musical

3 United States
AD College of Art
AG University Design Service, Carnegie
Mellon University
DIR Dennis Ichiyama
DES Maria Kyros
Lecture

4 Great Britain
AD National Film Theatre
AG Bloy Eldridge Design
DIR Neville Eldridge
DES Robert Custance
Film

5 Holland
DES Ralph Prins
Thirty years liberation

6 France
AD Musée d'Art Moderne
DES Roman Cièslewicz
Exhibition

7 Bulgaria
AD Ludmil Tcehlarov
AG Satiric Theatre
Play by Berthold Brecht

Poppentheater 'Guido van Deth'   Nassau Dillenburgstraat 8 Den Haag tel.070-249608

1

5

2

3

4

6

7

1 Holland
AD Gem. drukkerij Den Haag
DES Aart Verhoeven
Exhibition, Exposition

2 Italy
AD Council of Umbria
DES Michele Spera
Exhibition, Exposition

3 United States
AD Lenali
AG Artissimo Inc.
DIR/DES Tony Dispigna
Beauty boutique, Salon de beauté,
Kosmetiksalon

4 France
AD Bureau du Festival de Cannes
DIR/DES Georges Lacroix
Film festival

5 France
AD Loterie Nationale
DES Fix-Masseau
St Valentine's draw, La tranche Saint
Valentin, Lotterie

6a-c United States
AD Department of Music, Western
Michigan University
AG Design Center, Department of Art
DIR/DES Linda Powell
University cultural events, Programme
culturel d'une université, Kultur-
Programm einer Universität

7 Iran
AD Teheran University
DES H. Nowroozi
Theatre

8 Austria
AD Christl Dornbirn
AG Atelier Wiener
DIR Erich M. Wiener
Ties, Cravates, Kravatten

1

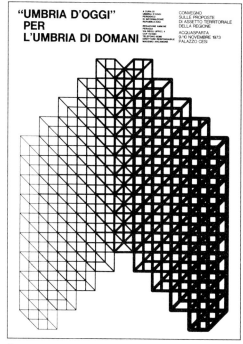

2

6a-c

3

4

5

7

8

Press advertisements
Annonces de presse
Zeitungs-Inserate

1a-c Holland
AD Het Nederlands Zuivelbureau
AG Prad B.V.
DIR Herman Gerritzen
ILL Jan M. Verburg
COPY Paul Mertz
Milk, Lait, Milch

1a-b

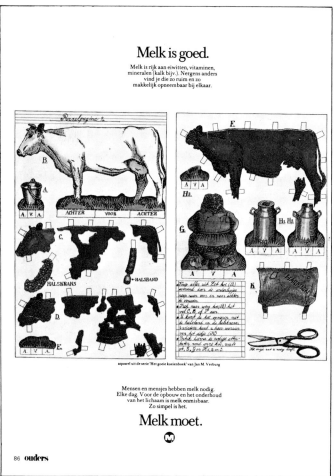

Melk is goed.

Melk is rijk aan eiwitten, vitaminen,
mineralen (kalk bijv.). Nergens anders
vind je die zo ruim en zo
makkelijk opneembaar bij elkaar.

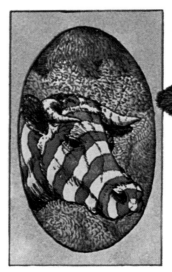

aquarel uit de serie 'Het goeie koeienboek' van Jan M. Verburg

Mensen en mensjes hebben melk nodig.
Elke dag. Voor de opbouw en het onderhoud
van het lichaam is melk onmisbaar.
Zo simpel is het.

Melk moet.

Avilon dyes for polyamide

In the dyeing of brushed nylon car upholstery
Avilon stands for

—good colour yield
—economy in use
—excellent all-round fastness, particularly
to light

CIBA—GEIGY
the natural choice in colour chemistry

Dyestuffs and Chemicals Division
CIBA-GEIGY (UK) Limited
Clayton Manchester
M11 4AR

1

à l'heure de la ménopause
ondogyne

ROUSSEL

2

4

5

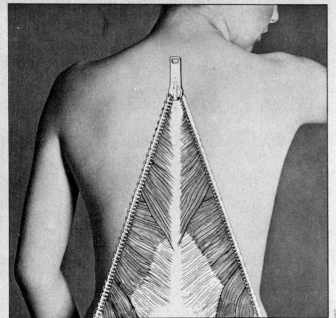

Dietro il dolore reumatico c'é sempre lo spasmo.
FLEXIDONE
libera dallo spasmo muscolare.

Il dolore reumatico causa sempre una contrattura muscolare, che dà origine al circolo vizioso dolore-spasmo-dolore.

FLEXIDONE, a base di carisoprodol e amidofenazone, libera da questa contrattura perché
produce un'azione miorilassante e analgesi-
ca (con il carisoprodol) oltre alla classica
azione degli antireumatici: antidolorifica, an-
tipiretica, antiessudativa, antistaminica (con
l'amidofenazone).

INDICAZIONI: Nelle lombalgie; artropatie degenerati-
ve e traumatiche (artrosi, sindromi discali, ecc.); tor-
cicollo; mioisti; mialgie; borsiti; fibrositi; nevralgie;
neviti; radicoliti; strappi e contusioni muscolari.

POSOLOGIA: Compresse: adulti 3-6 compresse nelle
24 ore (1-2 compresse ogni 8 ore); bambini 1-3 compresse nelle 24 ore (mezza - 1 compressa ogni 8 ore).
Supposte: adulti 2-3 supposte nelle 24 ore; bambini
1-2 supposte pediatriche nelle 24 ore.

INAM supposte adulti e pediatriche

FLEXIDONE
(carisoprodol + amidofenazone)

spezza il circolo vizioso
dolore-spasmo
spasmo-dolore

PIERREL

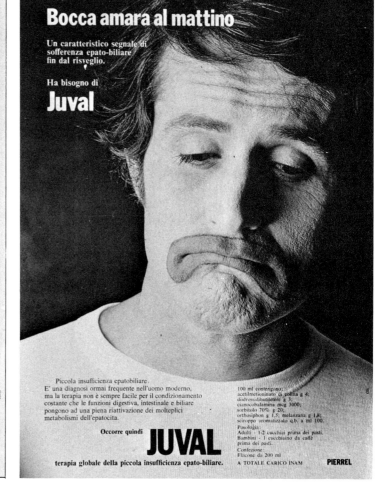

Bocca amara al mattino

Un caratteristico segnale di
sofferenza epato-biliare
fin dal risveglio.

Ha bisogno di
Juval

Piccola insufficienza epatobiliare.
E' una diagnosi ormai frequente nell'uomo moderno,
ma la terapia non è sempre facile per il condizionamento
costante che le funzioni digestiva, intestinale e biliare
pongono ad una piena riattivazione dei molteplici
metabolismi dell'epatocita.

Occorre quindi **JUVAL**
terapia globale della piccola insufficienza epato-biliare.

100 ml contengono:
acetilmetioninato di colina g 4;
diidrossidibutiletere g 3;
cianocobalamina mcg 3000;
sorbitolo 70% g 20;
orthosiphon g 1,5; melanzana g 1,8;
sciroppo aromatizzato q.b. a ml 100.
Posologia:
Adulti - 1-2 cucchiai prima dei pasti.
Bambini - 1 cucchiaino da caffè
prima dei pasti.
Confezione:
Flacone da 200 ml
A TOTALE CARICO INAM

PIERREL

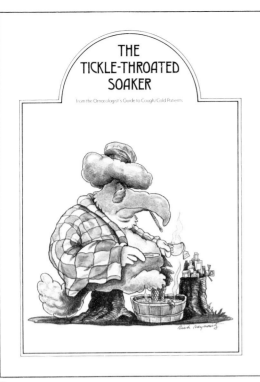

THE
TICKLE-THROATED
SOAKER

from the Ornacologist's Guide to Cough/Cold Patients

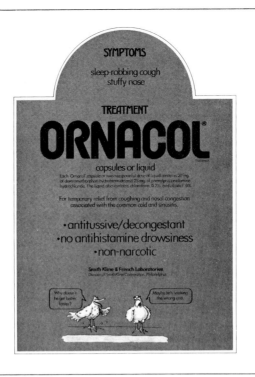

SYMPTOMS

sleep-robbing cough
stuffy nose

TREATMENT

ORNACOL®

capsules or liquid

Each Ornacol capsule or two teaspoonful doses of liquid contains 20 mg. of dextromethorphan hydrobromide and 25 mg. of phenylpropanolamine hydrochloride. The liquid also contains chloroform 0.2%, and alcohol 7.6%.

For temporary relief from coughing and nasal congestion associated with the common cold and sinusitis.

- antitussive/decongestant
- no antihistamine drowsiness
- non-narcotic

Smith Kline & French Laboratories
Division of SmithKline Corporation, Philadelphia

3

AFTER THE FLOOD CAME THE POLLEN

...even though man wasn't supposed to undergo any more worldwide disasters.

Yet every spring and fall, millions are victimized by the descendants of the first ragweed and its cousins.

Fortunately, man was resourceful.

And he brought forth an antihistaminic agent that, with time, has become a classic treatment for pollinosis: Benadryl (diphenhydramine HCl).

Despite the seemingly endless proliferation of antihistamines, Benadryl remains virtually synonymous with the effective treatment of hay fever symptoms: for prompt relief of sneezing, rhinorrhea, and itching eyes, nose and throat.

Supplied in 25-mg. capsules, 50-mg Kapseals®, Elixir, and Cream.

It's a much better solution than another flood.

THAT'S
WHY
MAN
INVENTED

BENADRYL®
(diphenhydramine HCl)
PARKE-DAVIS

Please see next page for prescribing information.

6

7

Sabendo usar, não vai faltar.

Este é um whisky especial.
Para máquinas muito especiais.
Um combustível de bom humor, para ser aplicado em pequenas doses, sem necessidade de se encher o tanque.
Uma pequena porção garante a energia necessária. Use-o sem exageros: o que é bom, dura muito.

Whisky Chequers

O escocês que levou mais de 130 anos para chegar ao Brasil:
"Chequers is now being despatched to all markets in restricted amount".

À venda na

Migros

A loja da luxúria, gula e tentação.
Rua Joaquim Floriano, 140 - Fone: 80-9904
Aberta até as 22 horas.

Bureau (d'après Agnelli)

Ett billigt sätt att bevara dyrbar mat.

Gladpack i stor rulle kostar
ca 6 öre halvmetern.
Vad maten kostar vet du bäst själv.

Ett billigt sätt att bevara dyrbar mat.

Gladpack i stor rulle kostar
ca 6 öre halvmetern.
Vad maten kostar vet du bäst själv.

1a-b

3a-b

Man kann manchmal schwarz sehen.

Man kann auch gleich rot sehen.

Man kann auch alles rosarot sehen.

Aber man kann auch alles so sehen, wie es wirklich ist.

Goldgelb und vollreif. Zartmürb und mildnussig.
Unser Emmentaler.
Wochenlang sorgsam gepflegt. Monatelang fach-
kundig gelagert.
Aus 12 Litern urgesunder Milch wurde 1 Kilo
urgesunder Emmentaler.
Energiegeladen, vitaminvoll, mineralreich. Gramm
für Gramm viel Kraft und Genuss. Für eigentlich
wenig Geld.
Das ist und bleibt unser Emmentaler.

 Viel Kraft und Genuss. Für wenig Geld. Emmentaler. Greyerzer. Sbrinz.   Schweizerische Käseunion AG. Bern

97

Für die Franzosen?

Für die Amerikaner?

Für die Japaner?

Für Alle.

Seit Jahrhunderten machen wir den Emmentaler nach
dem gleichen Rezept. Für die feinen Unterschiede sorgt
die Natur. Hat er etwa kirschengrosse Löcher und
schmeckt er vollaromatisch, reservieren wir ihn für die
Schweiz. Von dieser ausgesuchten Qualität sind das
8,5 Mio. kg. Die Amerikaner ziehen ihn vor, wenn die
Lochung spärlich, das Aroma leicht ist. Die Italiener
mögen ihn am liebsten mild und, speziell im Süden,
grossgelocht. (Nach Italien exportieren wir am meisten,
etwa 16 Mio. kg jährlich.) Aber Emmentaler bleibt
Emmentaler. Ob gross- oder kleingelocht, mild oder
rezent. Deshalb essen wir ihn alle gern.

 Das Gute liegt so nah: Greyerzer. Emmentaler. Sbrinz.   Schweizerische Käseunion AG. Bern

145

2a-b

1a-b Sweden
AD Union Carbide
AG Young & Rubicam AB
DIR/DES Anders Weinar
ILL Arne Nilsson
COPY Anders Weinar
Food wrap, Emballage pour aliments,
Lebensmittelverpackung

2a-b Germany
AD Greif-Farben
AG/DES Olaf Leu
ILL Goffin
Paints

3a-b Switzerland
AD Swiss Cheese Union Inc. Berne
AG Gisler & Gisler
DIR Fredy Steiner
PHOTO Marcel Hayoz
Cheese, Fromages, Käse

4 United States
AD Stuart Pharmaceuticals
AG Sudler & Hennessey, Inc.
DIR/DES Len Obsatz
PHOTO Carmine Macedonia
ILL Blake Hampton
COPY Diane Cooney, Bob Levine
Pharmaceuticals, Medikamente

5 Switzerland
AD Frau fashion magazine
DIR/DES Dieter Schmitz
Skiing clothes, Vêtements de ski,
Skikleider

4

5

Non solo le impronte digitali

Non solo quelle servono ad identificare una persona. Anche la distanza tra una pupilla e l'altra varia da individuo ad individuo, insieme ad altri dati antropometrici, che assommati, risultano differenti per ogni individuo, proprio come le impronte digitali. Quando un paio di occhiali esce dai nostri laboratori, noi abbiamo tenuto conto di tutto questo. Perciò non è più "un paio di occhiali" ma sono proprio i "vostri" occhiali.

Ottica **Antonelli**
del dott. Antonio Antonelli
LENTI A CONTATTO   MICROSCOPIA
70121 Bari via Dante, 67 telefono 232724

1

3

MEMORIA

5

Förkylningshals?
Bensokain hjälper mot halssmärtan!

Bensokain tabletter ACO är speciellt avsedda för smärtlindring i halsen. Varje tablett innehåller därför 5 mg bensokain. Dessutom ingår mentol, som ger tabletterna uppfriskande smak. Bensokain tabletter är fria från antibakteriella tillsatser.
Behandlingskostnaden med Bensokain tabletter är låg.

Förpackningar   Priser inkl. moms
20 st   2:70
50 st   4:80

Bensokain ACO
tabletter 5 mg

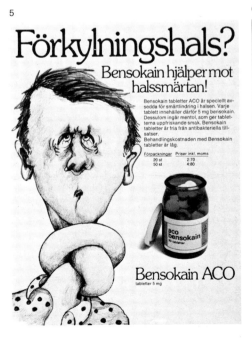

6

viaje seguro con repuestos legítimos
IKA·RENAULT

7

4

8

9

10

1 Italy
AD Ottica Antonelli Bari
AG/DES Mimmo Castellano
Optics

2 South Africa
AD Creamline Dairies
AG Jacques Lorraine Crystal
DIR/DES Tim Errill
PHOTO Fred Campy
Fruit juices, Jus de fruit, Fruchtsaft

3 Italy
AD Fometno de Obras y Construcciones
DIR R. Roda
DES D. Rubies
PHOTO C. Mas
Construction engineers

4 Holland
AD Seven-Up Nederland B.V.
AG Prad B.V.
DIR Dick van den Beemt
DES (dresses) Maarten Rodenberg
PHOTO Boudewijn Neuteboom
COPY Carli van Emde Boas
Soft drink and dresses, Boisson non-
alcoolique et robes, Getränke und
Kleider

5 Sweden
AD ACO
AG Gutenberghus
DIR P. O. Tjarnberg
ILL Jan Engström
Pharmaceuticals, Medikamente

6 Argentina
AD Ika-Renault
AG S. Freire
Car spares, Pièces détachées pour
voitures, Autoersatzteile

7 Switzerland
AD Addo AG
DIR Max Baltis
AG Werbeagentur MB & Co.
DES Heiri Scherer

8 Switzerland
AD Haldengut
AG Adolf Wirz AG
DIR H. Küste
DES J. Glaus
COPY F. Hunziker
Beer, Bière, Bier

9 Brazil
AD Coca-Cola
AG McCann Erickson
DIR/DES Vitor Lemos
PHOTO Francisco Pereira
COPY Gustavo Waenheldt
Christmas greetings

10 United States
AD Detroit News
AG Stevensessions Design
DIR/DES Steven Sessions
'Want' ads in newspaper, 'Want'
annonces dans un journal, 'Gesucht'
Inserat

Memories are made of this.

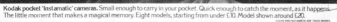

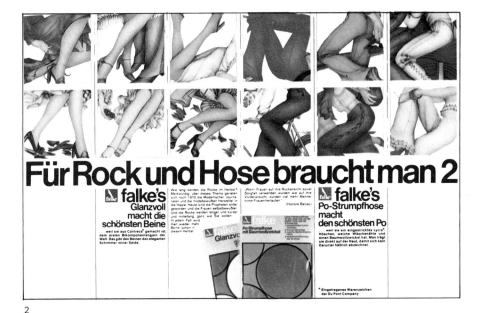

2

5

6

1 Italy
AD Triumph Swimsuits
AG Wirz AG
DIR Carlo Cavallini
DES Manfredi Vinassa de Regny
PHOTO Jean Daniel Lorieux
COPY Bruno Esposito
Insert for magazines

2 Germany
AD Falke
DES Barbara Buchwald
Panty hose

3 Great Britain
AD Kodak Ltd.
AG J. Walter Thompson
DIR/DES Peter Hughes
COPY Terry Howard

4 Germany
AD Fuji Photo Film (Europe) GmbH
AG EBD & CDP Werbeagentur
DIR Günter Bahr
ILL Christian von Alvensleben
Camera film

5 Switzerland
AD Swissair
AG Gerstner Gredinger Kuttner
Tourism

6 Germany
AD Fischer & Co.
DIR C. A. Froh
DES Peter Steiner
ILL N. C. Heinrich
Fashion, Anzeigen für Mode/
Tageszeitung

Le retour du "vrai" Hush Puppies.

Hush Puppies revient.
Avec ses grands yeux tristes et son air si sympathique,
tout le monde le reconnaîtra. Mais les chaussures ?

Seules les vraies Hush Puppies sont en peau de
porc tannée et traitée selon un procédé exclusif.
Ça leur permet de résister à tout, à l'usure
comme à la saleté. Et même aux chiens.

Les Hush Puppies sont doublées en peau de porc :
elles sont souples, légères, aérées, d'un confort
exceptionnel.

Les vraies Hush Puppies sont faciles à entretenir :
une bombe spéciale permet de les nettoyer
et de les raviver sans problème
(pour les chiens c'est plus difficile).

Enfin, les Hush Puppies sont d'un prix raisonnable
(nous ne savons pas ce qu'il en est pour les chiens).

Mais pour ne pas vous tromper, chez votre
marchand de chaussures, cherchez d'abord le chien :
lui, il est vraiment unique.

Hush Puppies®

125 F.

1

Quanto custa o material rodante? Cinco por cento do custo de um trator novo? Dez por cento do custo de um trator novo? Quinze por cento do custo de um trator novo? Vinte por cento do custo de um trator novo?

Além do material rodante ser extremamente caro, equivale a aproximadamente metade do custo total de manutenção da máquina.

E, já que ele é tão dispendioso, nós da Caterpillar queremos que você consiga reduzir ao máximo todos os seus custos com a manutenção da esteira.

Para isso, estamos continuamente pesquisando novos métodos que ajudem a diminuir o desgaste que ocorre no material rodante.

Assim, desenvolvemos os Retentores Duo-Cone, os vedadores de esteiras, introduzimos o aço de Endurecimento Profundo, e estamos trabalhando em outros equipamentos que possam reduzir ainda mais estes custos.

E os Revendedores Caterpillar, por sua vez, oferecem o S.E.M.R., Serviço Especializado do Material Rodante. Um serviço gratuito para todos os proprietários de tratores de esteiras Caterpillar.

Este serviço, consta de visitas regulares a cada máquina registrada, quando os especialistas de S.E.M.R. medem o desgaste do material rodante.

Assim, com os registros, é possível prever a melhor época para reparar ou substituir as peças do material rodante dentro do menor custo por hora.

E, seguindo as recomendações dos analistas do S.E.M.R., diversos contratempos na esteira podem ser localizados, antes que se transformem em sérias paralisações. Consulte o especialista de S.E.M.R., do seu Revendedor Caterpillar. Afinal, reduzindo os desgastes do material rodante, quem sai economizando é você.

Por falar nisto, o custo do material rodante equivale a 20% do custo de um trator novo.

CATERPILLAR

Caterpillar, Cat e ⫶B⫶ são marcas de Caterpillar Tractor Co.

Nossas máquinas constroem estradas perfeitas.
Quem as faz segura é você. Dirija com cuidado.

2

4

Wie immer, wann immer, warum immer
und wo immer Sie sich und den anderen
(hier: die andere) glücklich machen ...
zu den schönsten Augenblicken des
Lebens gehört immer ein bißchen
Einrichtung ...

„Bequemes Sitzen,
handwerkliches
Können und be-
stechendes Design
sind die Dinge,
die wir bei deSede
wichtig nehmen."
Urs Felber
deSede

Die Einrichtung WK

Leder-Polstermöbel der internationalen Spitzenklasse des schweizerischen Herstellers de Sede.
Neue Maßstäbe für schöneres, gesundes, bequemes Sitzen. Ausstellung 4. September bis 28. September 1974.
Die Einrichtung, Beringer u. Koettgen. Möbel, Innenausbau, Stoffe, Teppiche, Kunsthandwerk, Leuchten
8 München 2, Brienner Straße 12 und Wittelsbacher Platz 1, Telefon 2 30 91

5

Fabricando no Brasil os mesmos
fios que já ganharam o mundo.

CELANESE DO BRASIL

We see things from a child's point of view.

♦ Addison-Wesley
Publishing Company
Mathematics / Science / Social
Science / Language Arts / Reading
2725 Sand Hill Road
Menlo Park, California 94025

3

1 France
AD Hush Puppies
AG Mafia (Maimé Arnodin, Fayolle,
International Associés)
Shoes, Chaussures, Schuhe

2 Brazil
AD Caterpillar Brasil
AG Fator Publicidade
DIR Decio Duarte Ambrosio
DES Iranildo Alves da Silva
COPY Marcel Hirsch, Ernisto Klotzel
Technical support

3 United States
AD Addison-Wesley
AG Sam Smidt & Ass.
DIR/DES Paul Sinn
PHOTO Magnum
Educational programme

4 Germany
AD Die Einrichtung
AG Apollon
DIR/DES Lutz Roeder
ILL J. Harder, A. Hengstänberg,
M. Lazzeroni
Furniture, Meubles, Möbel

5 Brazil
AD Celanese do Brasil
AG Fator Publicidade
DIR Gesse Alves Pereira
COPY Dalton Pastore Jr., Ernesto Klotzel
Textiles

6a-b Holland
AD/AG Prad B.V.
DIR Herman Gerritzen
ILL Antoni Jensen
COPY Paul Mertz
Homage to the Danish artist Antoni
Jensen, Tribut für Antoni Jensen

6a-b

Einzigartige Komplimente.

Manchmal ist es so schwer, ihr zu sagen, was man für sie empfindet. Blumen, die welken. Und Worte – na ja. Doch da ist etwas, das eine Frau immer an das erinnert, was Sie ihr eigentlich sagen wollen, was genauso natürlich ist wie Blumen und genauso lieb wie ihre Worte – Diamantschmuck. Diamantschmuck – genau in dem Design, das zu ihr paßt wie ihre Lieblingsblume und genauso einzigartig ist wie ihre Stimme. Sollten Sie es ihr nicht vielleicht mal so sagen? Denn Diamanten sind Geschenke der Liebe, Anerkennung und Dankbarkeit.

DUGENA

1

Berliner Salat.

Man nehme: eine Stadt. Schneide sie hart an der Wurzel ab, übersprühe sie abwechselnd mit heißen und kalten Duschen, bis sie völlig abgebrüht ist. Löse dann Schale um Schale, bis nichts mehr übrigbleibt; vergesse nicht, kleinere und größere Krisen einzustreuen; füge zum Schluß noch ein paar Skandale hinzu und garniere das Ganze mit einer Prise vorgefaßter Meinung. Was bleibt, ist nicht wiederzuerkennen. Wem bekommt so etwas? Keinem. Also kommen Sie nach Berlin. Machen Sie sich Ihren eigenen Salat. Die Zutaten sind frisch und anregend wie am ersten Tag. **Wohl bekomm's.**

2

4

CAMPARI Orange

⅓ Campari. ⅔ Orangensaft. Dazu klirrendes Eis. Das ist Campari Orange. Eine neue Art, jederzeit Campari zu geniessen.

5

Mmmm . . . Mushroom and Tomato! Maybury's supreme blend

You'll love the exciting new flavour Maybury have created with your two all-time favourite soups, mushroom and tomato.

That delicious intangible flavour of freshly picked, earthy mushrooms. Blended with young, firm tomatoes and a hint of onion. Delicately spiced. Then creamed into thick, delectable broth.

It's the farm-fresh goodness of Mushroom and Tomato – and eight other heart-warming flavours – that makes Maybury soup night a family occasion. Every night. Maybury makes it.

MAYBURY FINE FOODS

Capture farm-fresh flavour in a can? Maybury can.

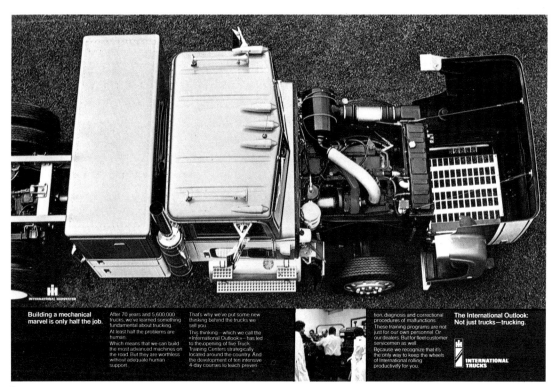

Building a mechanical marvel is only half the job.

After 70 years and 5,600,000 trucks, we've learned something fundamental about trucking.

At least half the problems are human.

Which means that we can build the most advanced machines on the road. But they are worthless without adequate human support.

That's why we've put some new thinking behind the trucks we sell you.

This thinking—which we call the «International Outlook»—has led to the opening of five Truck Training Centers strategically located around the country. And the development of ten intensive 4-day courses to teach preven-

tion, diagnosis and correctional procedures of malfunctions.

These training programs are not just for our own personnel. Or our dealers. But for fleet customer servicemen as well.

Because we recognize that it's the only way to keep the wheels of International rolling productively for you.

The International Outlook: Not just trucks—trucking.

INTERNATIONAL TRUCKS

3

ahh

GEVALIA

Du behöver bara känna doften för att veta varför Gevalia dricks mest.

6

How to smell a good wine when you taste one.

The Sunday Mail Color Magazine, December 2, 1973

ORLANDO

How to wrestle with a bottle of wine, and win.

The Sunday Mail Color Magazine, November 25, 1973

ORLANDO

1a-b

3

Huilen is voor jou te laat. Of niet?

4

ta´terminalen med Dem så er DD ved hånden

DD kører stærkt frem med terminaldrift

Terminaldrift åbner mulighed for en øget flexibilitet i anvendelsen af standard/rammesystemer på edb-servicebasis. - Specielt når dette kan kombineres med en transportabel terminal. Med en Silent 725 terminal fra Texas Instrument kan De udnytte DD's terminalmuligheder, hvor De end befinder Dem, blot der er adgang til en telefon. Silent 725 er udstyret med akustisk kobling og indbygget modem, d.v.a. datatransmissionen foregår direkte gennem telefonen uden normale startinvesteringer og lejeudgifter til installationer. Samtidig kan der gennem denne terminaltype og DD's timesharingsystem arbejdes med transmissionshastigheder, som er op til 3 gange hurtigere end ved brug af traditionelle TTY-terminaler. Dette betyder mindre opkoblet tid og reducerede telefonomkostninger. Yderligere giver DD's timesharingsystem

adgang til en række beregningsrutiner inden for områderne **administration og økonomi, operationsanalyse, konstruktionsteknik, statistik.** Her er bl.a. budgetsimuleringsprogrammet DØSS nu tilgængeligt. Dette program er resultatet af et netop offentliggjort projekt (Kåre Dullum, Henning Andersen og Flemming Rasmussen: Databehandlingsprogram for Økonomisk System Simulation. Samfundslitteratur 1974), hvor DD har stillet testtid til rådighed i slutfasen. DØSS har til formål at lette arbejdet med virksomhedens budgetter og langtidsplanlægning, hvor der bl.a. foretages beregninger af likviditet, overskudsudvikling m.v. Dette er typiske edb-opgaver, hvor den hurtige og direkte adgang til regnekapacitet er afgørende. DD's timesharingsystem kombineret med en transportabel terminal, løser problemet.

Hos DD kan De leje Silent 725 for en valgfri periode - og der er naturligvis ikke startomkostninger. Silent 725 indgår som naturligt led i en samlet terminal-løsning omfattende **timesharing, spørge-svar, remote batch.** En af vore konsulenter kommer gerne og uddyber terminalens muligheder.

D dansk dataservice as

DD Esbjerg Rotfsgade 122A, 6700 Esbjerg tlf. 05/13 58 17 / **DD Kolding** Vejlevej 159, 6000 Kolding tlf. 05/52 91 33 / **DD København** Energivej 30, 2750 Ballerup tlf. 01/97 25 33

2a-b

en trekantet nyhed fra DD

økonomistyringssystemet STANØKON

Kører den økonomiske styring på skinner i Deres virksomhed?
Så ved De, at det er et dynamisk område, hvor den løbende økonomiplanlægning hele tiden stiller krav til fleksibel rapportering, rullende budgetrevision og budgetkontrol.
De ved også, at det er et omkostningskrævende arbejde rent administrativt, da det ikke kan udføres af de almindelige kendte edb-systemer.
DD har med STANØKON skabt et seriøst alternativ til virksomhedsmedens nuværende administrative rutiner omkring økonomisk styring.
Resultatet er blevet et rammesystem, hvor uddata kan tilpasses den enkelte virksomheds ønsker og behov, og hvor standardsystemets sikkerhedsmæssige for-

dele og enkle indrapporteringsprocedure samtidig er bibeholdt.
Ideen bag STANØKON er illustreret i trekanten som systemets symbol. Den viser, at systemet er en genvej til et fuldt integreret informationssystem, incl. langtidsplanlægningsmodeller.
STANØKON's uddataside omfatter bl.a. rullende budgettering på kvartalsbasis, 12 måneders budgetoversigter, automatisk fordeling af årsbudgetter på de enkelte måneder og løbende udskrivning af forventet åresultat. De kan endvidere rekvirere engangsrapporter uafhængig af den faste kontoplan. STANØKON er det eneste økonomistyringssystem, der giver alle disse muligheder.
Samtidig arbejder systemet med et minimum af papir, det er prisbilligt og

kører dagligt med valgfri kørselsform. Vi er sikre på, at STANØKON er uundværligt for enhver virksomhed med mellem 25 og 500 ansatte.
En af vore konsulenter kommer gerne og uddyber systemets ide for Dem.

D dansk dataservice as

DD Esbjerg Englandsgade 12, 6700 Esbjerg tlf. 05/13 58 17 / **DD Kolding** Vejlevej 159, 6000 Kolding tlf. 05/52 91 33 / **DD København** Energivej 30, 2750 Ballerup tlf. 01/97 25 33

5

6

Wool travels boldly to the country in checks.
Takes to town in stylish flecks.
Whatever wool does it does it with flair.

Left: Andre Peters suit with longline check jacket and plain skirt, £42. Style 7136.

Right: Colin Glascoe two-piece with pleated skirt and tie neck shirt, £55. Co-ordinating tank top, £10. Style 1047. Prices are approximate.

 Pure new wool. There is nothing like it.

2b

Jedes Schaf hat von Geburt an ein Recht auf eine Klimaanlage.

Schurwolle wirkt wie eine automatische Klimaanlage, weil sie ihren eigenen Feuchtigkeitsgehalt stets der Umgebung anpaßt. Weil sie bei Feuchtigkeitsaufnahme Wärme freisetzt und weil sie bei Feuchtigkeitsabgabe Wärme verbraucht.

Das bedeutet: Kommen Sie z. B. im Winter mit Schurwoll-Kleidung aus einer warmen, trockenen Wohnung hinaus ins Kühle, Feuchte, nimmt die Schurwolle unmerkbar Feuchtigkeit auf - ohne sich feucht anzufühlen - und gibt dafür Wärme ab. Schurwolle hält also nicht nur warm, sondern wärmt auch selbst.

Kommen Sie aber in ein warmes, vielleicht sogar heißtrockenes Klima, gibt die Schurwoll-Kleidung Feuchtigkeit frei. Da bei diesem Vorgang Wärme verbraucht wird, entsteht durch

die sog. „Verdunstungskälte" ein angenehmer Kühlungseffekt. Diesen Klimaanlagen-Effekt kann sich jeder kaufen. Man braucht nur auf das Wollsiegel-Etikett zu achten.

Das Wollsiegel garantiert das Echte: Reine Schurwolle. Das Combi-Wollsiegel* garantiert eine gute Kombination: Schurwolle mit Beimischung.

Auf diese Gütezeichen (RAL) können Sie sich verlassen. Denn Wollsiegel-Qualität ist kontrollierte Qualität.

*Das Combi-Wollsiegel gibt es nur für bestimmte, dafür aber besonders geeignete Produktgruppen.

Das Echte — Reine Schurwolle
Eine gute Kombination — Schurwolle mit Beimischung

Wollsiegel-Qualität: Darauf können Sie sich verlassen.

4

さわやかウールの春がゆく。

吸湿性のよさが、素肌にさわやかな秘密です。
生きている繊維といわれるウール。これから汗ばんでくる季節には、吸湿性という鎧にせっせと精をだしはじめます。わたしたちのカラダの毛穴が閉じたり開いたりして体温を調節するのと同じように、スケールと呼ばれるウールの表皮が、外気の湿度の変化にあわせて、湿気を吸ったり、はいたりするのです。

もちろんこれは、目でみてわかるというものではありませんから、過去の経験などをちょっと思いだしてほしい。一見、涼しげにみえた服なのに、どうにも暑くてやりきれなかったということ、ありませんか。その点ウール自体の重さのものの湿気を吸ったときでも、全然ベタつく感じがしない。そのうえ繊維の外にどんどん温気がぬけるため、自然の妙をそなえているため、カラダがムレることもなく、いつもさわやかな肌ざわりなのです。

軽くて軽い、シャリ感がある。さわやかウール。
これからのワードローブにあと一つ、どうしてもかかせないもの、それはウキウキしてくる春のこなしにふさわしい優しさです。
そのために、できるだけ薄く、軽くしたものがさわやかウール。これは、ウールの繊維そのものが豊かな弾力性をそなえているからこそ、できることです。ドレープのゆたうような美しさも大切なファッション要素のひとつですものね。
国際羊毛事務局、東京都渋谷区本版局内区

Big walk
Big wool

ウール・マークは、世界34か国で使用されているウールのマーク。証明した一つのウール商品は●新£100パーセント (ALL NEW WOOL) であり ●商品につけられた一定の品質基準のもとに管理されています。

5

1 Italy
AD International Wool Secretariat
AG ODG
DIR R. Damioli
New wool

2a-b Great Britain
AD International Wool Secretariat, London
AG Davidson, Pearce, Barry & Spottiswoode
DIR/DES Brian Bridge
PHOTO Eva Sereny (a)
        Duffy (b)
COPY Jill Asquith

3 France
AD International Wool Secretariat, Paris
AG Feldmann, Calleux Associés
DIR Bruno Suter
PHOTO Giles Bensimon

4 Germany
AD International Wool Secretariat, Düsseldorf
AG Troost Werbeagentur

5 Japan
AD International Wool Secretariat, Tokyo

JUST THINK, FOR A FEW PENCE LESS YOU CAN HAVE ONE THAT CRACKLES, HISSES, SPLUTTERS, & FINALLY JAMS.

1

Mit Zanders mehr Zeit für das, was zählt

2a-b

4

Sempers nya leksaker för leksugna i olika åldrar.

Ringskallran 0 till 6 mån

Ringpyramiden 1½ till 2½ år

Bultlådan 1½ till 3 år

Klosslådan 1½ till 5 år

Stormosaik från 4 år

Bokstavsklossar 5 till 8 år

Lär känna din kropp 6 till 10 år

lek som lär: 1½ till 5 år
Klosslådan

5

We don't let a spot of bad luck keep you off the road.

Keep Motoring. Honestly, it's the best policy.

the holidaymakers are changing

We've been making happy holidays for many people for a long time now. That's why people call us The Holidaymakers.

But we're making a few changes at Premier this year.

To start with our regional network of Premier Travel Centres has a new look. A brighter look with a new orange and brown symbol which reflects the resources of one of Anglia's largest travel organisations. Resources which follow you every step of the way whether you are a tourist to Torremolinos, a businessman to Bangkok or a

charter group to Guatemala.

It is certainly something worth looking for since it can be your guarantee of the care and attention which Premier Travel Centres give to all your travel requirements.

Bigger and better

Not only are we looking good. This year with two new travel centres in our 15-strong network, we are now even more widespread.

But such growth and development (which incidentally is reflected through our other travel operations involved in scheduled coach services and

our own British tours programme) needs more than a new symbol to help us cope with the increased demands for our services. So we've made other changes like gearing-up our behind-the-scenes administration. Increasing our staff to allow more time for us to cover the world searching and looking. Seeking new destinations; looking at new hotels; sampling the food, the climate and the facilities. Appointing our own training officer to train our staff to look after you better. Checking the currency and the prices. All this before we feel ready to come back and talk to you about it.

You see we are now bigger, better and even brighter. Just keep a look-out for the 'new-look' Premier Travel. We're sure you'll see the difference.

Premier Travel Agency Ltd
Rose Crescent, Cambridge
Telephone (0223) 64231

Also at: Saffron Walden, Royston, Ely, Huntingdon, Letchworth, Ware, Peterborough, Bedford, St. Ives, Haverhill, Mildenhall, Ramsey and Halstead.

Premier Travel Agency. The Holidaymakers

3

6

Feuer

Wildschaden

Glasbruch

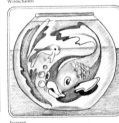
Insassen

Haftpflicht

Steinschlag

... gegen Papierkrieg

Parkschaden

Diebstahl

Bei Avis sind Sie sicher,
dass Sie richtig versichert sind.

Bei Avis sind Sie sicher, ein sicheres Auto zu fahren. Nicht nur, weil alle Avis-Wagen praktisch neu sind, sondern auch, weil alle Avis-Wagen vor jeder Fahrt auf Herz und Nieren geprüft werden. Mit strassenverkehrsamtlicher Gründlichkeit.

Aber auch mit dem sichersten Auto kann etwas passieren. Darum muss es versichert werden. Und zwar so, dass Sie als Mieter – geschehe, was wolle – weder Ärger noch Kosten haben. Gegen die Kosten schützen Sie unsere unbegrenzte Haftpflichtversicherung (ohne Selbstbehalt!) und der volle Versicherungsschutz bei Feuer, Elementarschäden, Glasbruch und Diebstahl. Gegen den Ärger schützt Sie ein besonderer Kundendienst von Avis: Wenn Sie

in einen Unfall verwickelt werden, stellt Ihnen Avis sofort einen Ersatzwagen.

Das alles mag genügen – und genügt oft nicht. Darum besprechen wir mit jedem Kunden, ob sich für ihn eine Zusatzversicherung empfiehlt. Vollkasko ohne Selbstbehalt zum Beispiel; oder eine Insassenversicherung für den Fahrer selbst oder, wenn er jemanden mitnehmen will; oder eine Transportgutversicherung (bei Transportern), wenn er etwas Wertvolles transportieren will. Alles gegen eine geringe Gebühr. Aber dafür kann er sicher sein, voll und richtig versichert zu sein.

Sie finden uns an 2500 Avis-Stationen auf der ganzen Welt; oder an 45 Stationen in der ganzen Schweiz. Sie finden bei uns 30 verschiedene PW-Modelle und 15 verschiedene Transporter-Modelle. Und Sie finden bei uns Tarife, die Ihnen manches ersparen können.

Bitte informieren Sie mich ausführlicher über Avis-Stationen und -Leistungen.

Name

Strasse

PLZ/Ort

Geburtsdatum

Senden an: Avis, Flughofstr. 61, 8152 Glattbrugg

Avis
Autovermietung

Wir vermieten neue Chrysler, viele andere und auch Nutzfahrzeuge.

1 Great Britain
AD BASF United Kingdom Ltd.
AG Maisey, Mukerjee, Russell
DIR/DES Bill Thompson
ILL Ed White
Cassettes

2a-b Germany
AD Zanders Feinpapier GmbH
AG Creativ-Team-Berlin
Paper

3 Great Britain
AD Premier Travel Agency
AG Ken Vail Graphic Design
DES Ken Vail
COPY Barry Hook
Travel agency, Agence de voyage,
Reisebureau

4 Sweden
AD Semper AB
AG Lenskog & Co.
DIR/DES Kenneth Bodlund
PHOTO Janne Bengtsson
ILL Rolf Sjödin
COPY Steve Trygg
Educational toys, Jouets éducatifs,
Pädagogische Spielzeuge

5 Great Britain
AD General Accident
AG Leo Burnett Ltd.
DIR Chris Morling
PHOTO Bob Hubbard
Motor insurance, Assurance automobile,
Fahrzeugversicherung

6 Switzerland
AD Avis
AG Adolf Wirz AG
DIR/DES M. Willuweit
COPY R. Biedermann
Motor insurance, Assurance automobile,
Fahrzeugversicherung

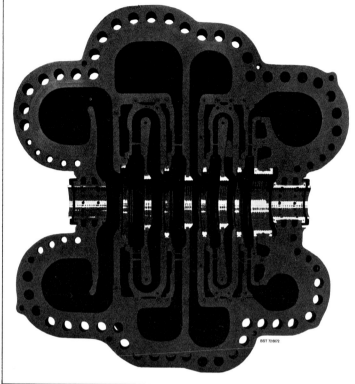

1 Germany
AD Deutsche Verlags-Anstalt Stuttgart
DES Dieter Zembsch
Book publicity, Buchwerbung

2 Germany
AD Brown Boveri-Sulzer
DES G. A. Weidig
ILL Walter Spahn
Turbocompressors

3 Spain
AD/AG Carlos Rolando & Asociados
DIR/DES C. Rolando
ILL Daniel Melgarejo
Self-promotion for trade magazine,
Promotion individuelle de revue
spécialisée

4 United States
AD Syntex
AG Sam Smidt & Associates
DIR/DES Paul Sinn
ILL Nick Pavloff
COPY Perry Leftwich
Pharmaceuticals, Medikamente

5 Israel
AD Tnuva Tel-Aviv
AG Arieli Ltd.
DES Ilana Steinitz-Richardson
Dairy products, Fromage, Käse-produkte

6 South Africa
AD Creamline Dairies
AG Jacques Lorraine Crystal
DIR/DES Bruce Backhouse
PHOTO Chris Webster
Yoghurt

7a-b United States
AD Mobil Oil Corporation
AG Chermayeff & Geismar Associates
DIR/DES Ivan Chermayeff
TV promotion

3

7a-b

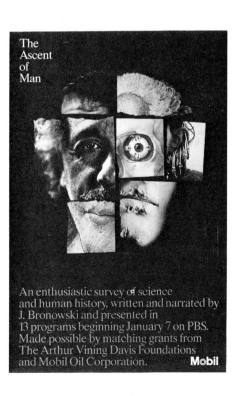

Watch Elgin Watch.

The kind of thinking that made
Elgin famous in the first place
is back in action again.
But we aren't going to rest on
our unbreakable mainspring.
Among other things, we're
introducing a new solid-state
digital. A new electronic day-date.
A new ladies' quartz.
Things are set to happen in the
next few months that will set
this industry on its ear.
Good things, if you're with us.
If you're not, watch out.

ELGIN WATCH Things are ticking again.

Elgin Watch, 570 West Jackson Blvd, Chicago, Il. 60606

3

5

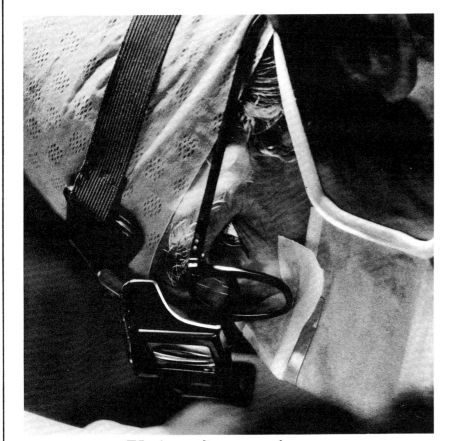

Vedere è prevedere.
Noi diamo più occhi alla vostra azienda.

Chiave del vostro futuro sono i fatti del vostro presente. Più occhi vuol dire più conoscenza. Più visione. Più dati. Più informazione.

Informazione in chiaro. Informazione scritta. Informazione direttamente al tavolo in cui si lavora e si decide. E subito. Noi produciamo gli strumenti per produrla.

Indipendentemente dai linguaggi: parole o numeri. Indipendentemente dalle tecnologie: microcomputer o terminali, sistemi di elaborazione contabile o macchine copiatrici. E software per tutte le vostre specifiche applicazioni.

Vedere per prevedere. In un mondo incerto è questo

il problema dei problemi: aiutarvi a risolverlo è il nostro mestiere.

OLIVETTI SISTEMI E SOFTWARE PER L'INFORMAZIONE

Sistemi per raccolta, trasmissione e trattamento dati.
Macchine e sistemi per contabilità e amministrazione.
Macchine per copiare.
Microcomputer e calcolatrici elettroniche scriventi.
Sistemi elettronici di scrittura e macchine per scrivere.

olivetti

1 Switzerland
AD Atlantis Hotel
AG Adolf Wirz AG
DIR/DES A. Bosshard
ILL A. Schuppisser
COPY H. Höfler
Hotel

2 Great Britain
AD B. H. Morris & Co. Ltd.
AG Maisey, Mukerjee, Russell
DIR/DES Gary Denham
ILL Max Forsythe
Stereo systems

3 United States
AD Elgin Watch
AG BBDM, Inc.
DIR/DES Gary P. Melzer
ILL Victor Skrebneski
COPY Todd D. Lief
Watches

4 Canada
AD Jules Fine Enterprises Ltd.
AG Raymond Lee & Associates Ltd.
DIR Richard Hone
DES Richard Hone, John Dymun
ILL Viktor von Madespach
COPY John Dymun
Restaurant

5 Italy
AD Ing. C. Olivetti & Co., S.p.A.
AG DRCDIP/S.P.P.
DIR/DES Giovanni Ferioli
PHOTO Romano Cagnoni
COPY Giovanni Giudici

Typefaces

Caractères

Schrifttypen

Bookjackets

Chemises de Livres

Buchumschläge

1 Iran
AD Institute for the Intellectual
Development of Children and Young
Adults
ILL Nafiseh Riahi

2 Germany
AD/AG H. Berthold AG
DIR Götz Gunnar Gorissen
DES Wolfgang Schulze
Type Specimen Book

1

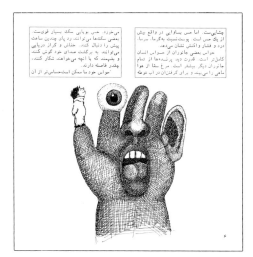

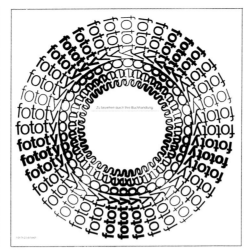

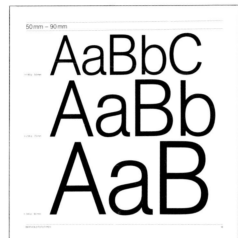
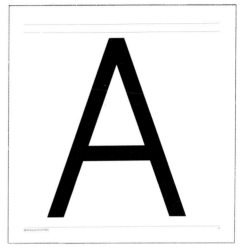
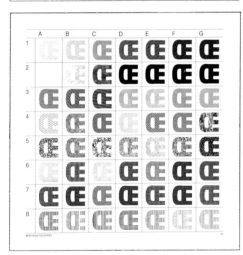

AABBCD
EFGHIJJ
KLMNNO
PQRSTT
UUVW
XYZ
&
0123456789

abcde
fghijklmn
opqrstu
vwxyz
ffifl,
ſß.
&
0123456789

abcdefghijklmnopqrstuvwxyz
ææøø¢||"';.,!? 1234567890

American Typewriter Outline

abcdeefghijklmnopqrstuvwxyz
ABCDEFGHIJKLMNOPQRSTUVWXYZ
1234567890 (&&.,:;!?'""–—[]*$$¢%/£@#)

American Typewriter Bold

abcdeefghijklmnopqrstuvwxyz
ABCDEFGHIJKLMNOPQRSTUVWXYZ
1234567890 (&&.,:;!?'""–—[]*$$¢%/£@#)

abcdefghijklmnop
qrstuvwxyz

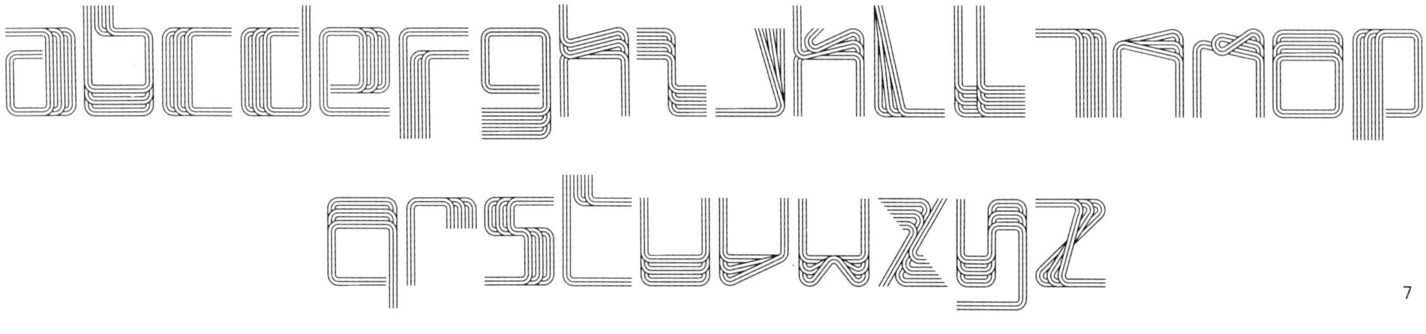

2

4

ΑΒΓΔΕΖΗΘΙΪΚΛΜΝΞΟΠΡϹΤΥΦΧΨΩΩϤϦϪϪϪΧϬϯϹ

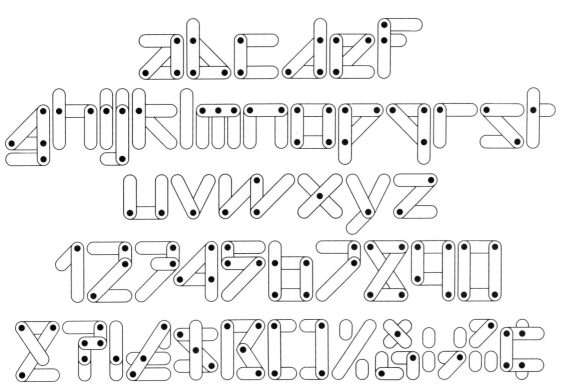

6

8

ΑΒΓΔΗΟΖΗΤΙΚΛΜΜΝΟΥ
0987654321ΥΡΥΥΥΥΥΥ

Typefaces
Caractères
Schrifttypen

1a-b France
AD Letraset
DIR/DES François Boltana
Typeface 'Stilla', Caractères 'Stilla',
Druckschrift 'Stilla' ©

2 Japan
AD Shaken
DIR Masakatsu Suga
DES Minotu Tanimichi
©

3 Great Britain
AD Mecanorma (Letterpress)
AG Bruce D. Stainsby Graphic Design
DES Bruce D. Stainsby
New typeface 'Blowfly', Nouveau
caractère 'Blowfly', Neue Druckschrift
'Blowfly' ©

4 Holland
AD Printing Office Orientaliste
DES Chris Brand
Dragnet Coptic ©

5 United States
AD Visual Graphics Corp.
AG In-House
DIR/DES B. Gary Kramig
ILL Bob Deguise
COPY Eli Barry
New typefaces, Nouveaux caractères,
Neue Druckschrift ©

6 United States
AD Photo Lettering Inc.
DES Rinaldo Cutini
New alphabet 'Meccano'. Patent
pending in the USA. All rights reserved
to Photo Lettering ©, Nouvel alphabet
'Meccano'. Brevet en attente aux USA.
Tous droits réservés à Photo Lettering ©,
Neue Druckschrift 'Meccano'. Im
Begriff, patentiert zu werden in USA.
Alle Rechte vorbehalten by Photo
Lettering ©

7 Venezuela
AD Museo de Arte Contemporaneo
DES M. F. Nedo
Alphabet for the museum, Alphabet
pour musée, Druckschrift für das
Museum ©

8 Israel
AD/DES Asher Oron
New typeface, Nouveau caractère,
Neue Druckschrift ©

phototitrage

ABCÇDEFGHIJKLMNOPQRSTUI123456 menhir (j. larcher)
ABCÇDEEFGHIJKLMNOPQRSTUI234567 menhir 8 (j. larcher)
ABCDEEFGHIJKLMNOPQRI234567890 menhir 6 (j. larcher)
ABCDEEFGHIJKLMNOPQRSTI2345678 menhir 4 (j. larcher)
ABCDEFGHIJKLMNOPQRSTI12345 regamey (a. regamey)
ABCÇDEFGHIJKLMNOP1234567890 bronx noir (m. waxmann)
ABCÇDEFGHIJKLMNOPQRSTUV123456 bronx noir étroit (m. waxmann)
ABCÇDEFGHIJKLMNOPQR12345O bronx shadow étroit (m. waxmann)
ABCÇDEFGHIJKLMN1234567890 bronx shadow (m. waxmann)
ABCDEFGHIJKLMNOP1234567O bronx ombré (m. waxmann)
ABCÇDEFGHIJKLMNOPQ1234567 bronx éclairé (m. waxmann)
abcdefghijklmnopqrstuv1234567890 valérie light (f. schneider)
ABCDEFGHIJKLMNOPQRSTUVWXYZ
abcdefghijklmnopqrstuvwxyz12345678 valérie médium (f. schneider)
ABCDEFGHIJKLMNOPQRSTUVWXYZ
abcdefghijklmnopqrstui1234567890 valérie bold (f. schneider)
ABCDEFGHIJKLMNOPQRSTUVWXYZ
abcdefghijklmnopqrstuvwxyz12345678 valérie black (f. schneider)
ABCDEFGHIJKLMNOPQRSTUVWXYZ

ABCÇDEFGHIJKLMNOPQR12345 hot-dog (j.-m. collas)
abcdeefghijjjkllll mnopqrst123456789 tok (m. poteau)
ABCDEFGHIJKLMNOPQRSTUVWXYZ1234567 8 françois éclairé (c. marchal)
abcdefghijklmnopqrstuvwxyz123456 michel éclairé (m. waxmann)
ABCDEFGHIJKLMNOPQRSTUVWXYZ
ABCDEFGHIJKLMNOPQR12345 guapo outline (j. larcher)
abcçdefghijklmnop1234567890 guapo shaded (j. larcher)
ABCÇDEFGHIJKLMNOPQR1234 guapo black shaded (j. larcher)
ABCÇDEFGHIJKLMNOP123456 guapo black (j. larcher)
abcdefghijklmnopqrstuvwxyz123456789o soleil (j. larcher)
ABCDEFGHIJKLMNOPQRSTUVWXYZ
ABCÇDEFGHIJKLMNOPQRSTUVI234567 gobelin (j. lapierre)
ABCDEFGHIJKLMNOPQRSTUVWXYZ123456789o larcher (j. larcher)
abcdefghijklmnopqrstuvwxyz1234567890 furtwangler (j.-c. bey)
ABCÇDEFGHIJKLMNOPQRSTUV123456789 stanislas (a. regamey)
abcçdefghijklmnopqrstuvwxyz1234567890 lapierre (j. lapierre)
ABCÇDEFGHIJKLMNOPQRSTUVWXYZ
abcdefghijklmn12345678 golf (f. doyonnax)

abcdefghijklmnopqrstuvwxyz1234567890 oxford
abcdefghijklmnopqrstuvwxyz1234567890 oxford inline
abcdefghijklmnopqrstuvwxyz1234567890 oxford outline
ABCDEFGHIJKLMNOPI234567890 black line
abcdefghijklmnopqrstuvw1234567890
AABBCTDDEEFFGGHHIIJJKKLLM archie

1

3a

3b

o biancofiore simbol d'amore
di Nerone
mani nere
e cuor d'oro
l'umor nero
Chiara
rimembri ancora
in Dattilo
NERISSIMO

pantera nera
nella sonate
al chiaro di luna
sulle rive del
mar nero era
una notte nera nera
come il carbon
in Dattilo
NERISSIMO

nera aristocrazia di sceicchi
au clair de la lune
mon ami Pierrot
Inferno pregiato vino
da uve nere
el negro Zombon
Black Power
in Dattilo
NERISSIMO

chiaroscuro delicate
nella notte buja
Nero Wolfe
rischiara nel tunnel
noir d'hivoire
Schwarzenbach
per Ilio Negri
in Dattilo
NERISSIMO

4

transotype 2000/Neuzeit Grotesk

Konturen

2a-b

Fotosatz Titelschriften

Caractères pour phototitrage Caratteri per fototitolatura Typefaces for display photosetting

Typefaces
Caractères
Schrifttypen

1 France
AD Hollenstein Phototypo
DIR/DES Albert Hollenstein
Services of type studio, Type
prospectus ©

2a-c Switzerland
AD Gloor Satz Repro
DIR Ernst Gloor
DES Bert Aureli, Werner Speich
Type specimens ©

3a-b Italy
AD Societa Nebiolo
DIR G. Iliprandi
DES Piero de Macchi (a)
ILL G. Iliprandi (b)
Typeface promotion, Promotion d'un
caractère ©

4 Germany
AD/AG Transotype Herman Holtz
Instant-lettering catalogue ©

5a-c Germany
AD D. Stempel AG
DIR/DES Erich Schulz-Anker
Type specimens, Druckschriften
(Handsatztypen) ©

GILK 22
Gilkon 27
Gilko 23
Gilko 28
GILK 24
Gilkon 29
GILK 25
GILK 30
GILKO 26
GILK 31

2c

5a-c

Universal-
Schriftprobe

Specimen
des Caractères

Specimen Book
of Typefaces

Stempel
Haas

Erläuterungen
Explications
General Remarks

Teil
Part

Antiqua-Schriften
Caractères Romains
Romans — 1

Serifenlose Schriften
Caractères Antiques
Sans Serifs — 2

Serifenbetonte Schriften
Caractères Égyptiennes
Slab Serifs — 3

Schreibschriften
Caractères Écritures
Scripts — 4

Sonstige Schriften
Caractères divers
Others
Antiqua-Varianten
Gebrochene Schriften
Schreibmaschinenschriften
Fremde Schriften — 5

Linotype-Versionen
Caractères à main Linotype
Linotype Versions — 6

Times Antiqua normal

6 Zu dem Glanzpunkt des idyllischen Viertels am See gehören die Grünanlagen und Gärten
7 Basel-Mulhouse, der einzige internationale Flughafen, der drei Ländern dient
8 Singapour, le grand port animé, l'aventure, la perle de choix, riche et fière
9 Sail-fish are found in the Atlantic, the Pacific and the Indian Oceans
10 Ceylon, die Insel, die einem einzigen tropischen Garten gleicht
11 Che bel contrasto tra il verde chiaro delle foglie e le arance
12 Die Küstenstraße führt zu den Ruinen Karthagos
14 Particulier à chaque catégorie de commerçants
16 Ein Lager wurde für das Fest aufgebaut
18 Dansk·Boghåndværk København
20 Interessanter Film über Afrika
22 Reklame komt U ten goede
24 Feux de joie sur la Marne
28 A Trip to the Glacier
36 Flughafenservice
48 Télégramme
60 Schönheit
72 Konzert

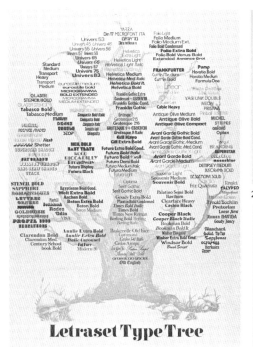

Letraset Type Tree

1

2

3

Letraset information

5

LETRAGRAPHICA 16, 17 AND 18

Letraset usa inc.

6a

6b

Letraset

9a

9b

letraline

8

Letraset

10a

Helvetica Medium

ABCDEFGHIJKLMNOPQRSTUVWXYZ
abcdefghijklmnopqrstuvwxyz
1234567890
&?!ß£$()¼½¾%

46

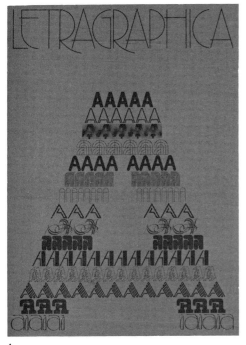

4

7

11a

12

11b

Bookjackets
Chemises de livres
Buchumschläge

1

2

3a

6

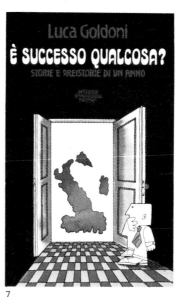

7

12

13

3b

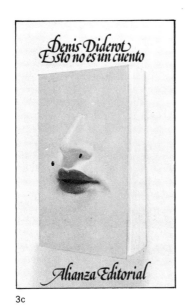

3c

4

5

9

10

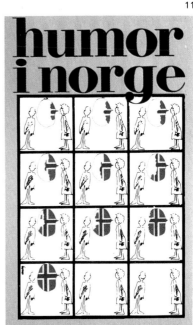

11

16

14

15

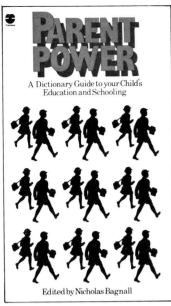

1

2

3

4

8

9

10

14

15

16

17

5

11

6

12

7

13

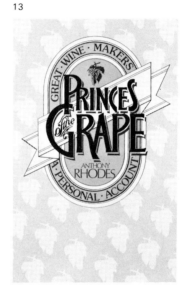

1 Great Britain
AD Fontana Books
DES Ken Carroll

2 Germany
AD Fischer Taschenbücher
DES Klaus Endrikat

3 Germany
Fischer Taschenbücher
DES Jan Buchholz, Reni Hinsch

4 Spain
AD Editorial Planeta
AG Carlos Rolando & Asociados
DIR/DES C. Rolando
ILL C. Rolando, Daniel Melgarejo

5 Great Britain
AD Fontana Books
DES Tad Aronowicz

6 Great Britain
AD W. H. Allen
DIR John Munday
DES/ILL Roman Buj

7 United States
AD Doubleday and Co.
AG Wendell Minor Design
DIR Alex Gotfryd
DES/ILL Wendell Minor

8 Germany
AD Büchergilde Gutenberg
DIR Jürgen Seuss
DES Erhard Göttlicher
Desmond Bagley

9 Argentina
AD Eudeba — Editorial Universitaria de Buenos Aires
AG Departamento di Arte
DIR Ricardo Ducasse
DES Jorge A. Canale

10 Sweden
AD Zindermans Förlag
DES/ILL Kjell Ivan Anderson

11 Australia
AD The Macmillan Co. of Australia
AG Cato Hibberd Hawksby Pty. Ltd.
ILL John Pollard

12 Bulgaria
AD 'Narodna Kultura'
DES Cyril Gogov
Czech and Slovakian poets

13 Great Britain
AD Weidenfeld and Nicolson
DIR James Campus
DES Nick Sutton

14 Italy
AD Feltrinelli Editore
AG Studio Coppola
DIR/DES Silvio Coppola

15 Germany
AD Eulenspiegel-Verlag
DES Renate and Egbert Herfurth

18

Leo Tolstoj
Wieviel Erde braucht der Mensch?

16 Germany
AD Rowohlt Verlag
DIR/DES Dieter Ziegenfeuter

17 Great Britain
AD Barrie and Jenkins
DES Michael Codd

18 Germany
AD Büchergilde Gutenberg
DES Michael Mathias Prechtl

Sentence book L-Z

ESA Creative Learning Ltd

1a-b

O o

Oliver owns an ostrich

The ostrich was an old one

6

Richard Mabey
Food for Free
A guide to the edible wild plants of Britain

2

The Senses
TOUCH
Arthur Nicholls

7

Imagine you're English
D. Gibbs   N. Goodey

5

Belin

8

מדריך טלפון תשל"ד 1974

10

242 ST-B'WAY
SOUTH FERRY
BROADWAY LOCAL

Watching my name go by
Documented by Mervyn Kurlansky & Jon Naar. Text by Norman Mailer

11

Heije Faber
RELIGIONS PSYCHOLOGIE

12

MARILYN FERGUSON
LA REVOLUTION DU CERVEAU

CALMANN-LEVY

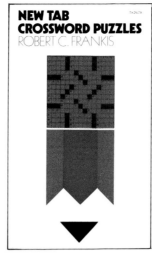

3

4

5

9a-b

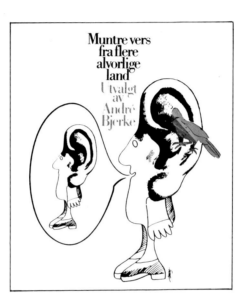

13

14

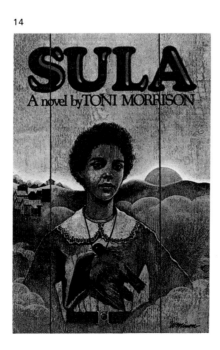

1a-b Great Britain
AD ESA Creative Learning Ltd.
DES Ron van der Meer
Teaching programme, Programme
d'éducation, Lehrprogramm

2 Great Britain
AD Fontana Books
DES Tony Evans

3 Great Britain
AD Fontana Books
DES Michael Dempsey

4 Germany
AD Fischer Taschenbuch Verlag
DES Jan Buchholz, Reni Hinsch

5 United States
AD Scholastic Books
AG Barnett/Goslin/Barnett
DIR Bob Feldgus, Dennis Barnett
DES Charles Goslin

6 Great Britain
AD Studio Vista
AG Flax & Kingsnorth

7 France
AD Belin
AG Orange
DIR/DES Philip Oldfield
English language book, Englisches
Lehrbuch

8 Israel
AD Ministry of Communications of Israel
AG KV Design International
DIR A. Kalderon
DES Asher Kalderon, Ester Kurty
Telephone book

9a-b Norway
AD Den Norske Bokklubben
DES Hansjørgen Toming
ILL Beth Toming

10 Great Britain
AD/AG Pentagram Design Partnership
DIR/DES Mervyn Kurlansky
ILL Jon Naar

11 Germany
AD Gütersloher Verlagshaus
DIR H. J. Heurer
DES Peter Steiner
The psychology of religion, Psychologie
religieuse, Die Psychologie der Religion

12 France
AD Calmann-Lévy
AG Graphic and Co.
DIR F. Schweblin
DES/ILL P. Courivaud

13 Great Britain
AD National Portrait Gallery
AG HMSO Graphic Design
DIR/DES Barrie Jones
COPY Eileen Harris
Catalogue of illustrations, Catalogue
des illustrations, Ein Katalog von
Illustrationen

14 United States
AD Alfred A. Knopf
AG Wendell Minor Design
DIR Bob Scudellari
DES Wendell Minor

Fernseheule

83

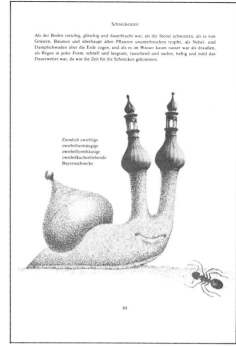

Schneckenzeit

Als der Boden rutschig, glitschig und dauerfeucht war, als die Steine schwitzten, als es von Gräsern, Bäumen und überhaupt allen Pflanzen ununterbrochen tropfte, als Nebel- und Dampfschwaden über die Erde zogen, und als es im Wasser kaum nasser war als draußen, als Regen in jeder Form, schnell und langsam, rauschend und sachte, heftig und mild das Dauerwetter war, da war die Zeit für die Schnecken gekommen.

Ziemlich zwieblige
zwiebelturmäugige
zwiebelformhäusige
zwiebelkuchenliebende
Bayernschnecke

89

1a-c

4

5

8a-b

2

3

6

7

9

10

1a-c Germany
AD Beltz & Gelberg
DES Günther Stiller
ILL Dieter Brembs

2 Sweden
AD Mölnlycke Hygien
AG Fältman & Malmén AB
DIR Gunnar Fältman
DES Lars Melander
Sex-education

3 Norway
AD Statens Informasjons Tjeneste
DES Paul Brand
Education programme

4 Sweden
AD Almänna Förlagat
DES Ronald Klang

5 Germany
AD Heidmück Verlag
DIR Günther U. Müller
DES Eva-Maria Ott-Heidmann

6 Great Britain
AD Frederick Warne
DES Harold King
ILL John Astrop

7 Great Britain
AD Robson Books
DES Timothy Jaques

8a-b Great Britain
AD Angus & Robertson
DIR Peter Loveday
ILL Agnes Molnar

9 India
AD Vikas Publishing House
DIR/ILL Aravind Teki
DES Man Mohan

10 Iran
AD Toos Publishing House
AG Tarh Studio
DIR/DES H. Nowroozi
Cazacks stories for children

1

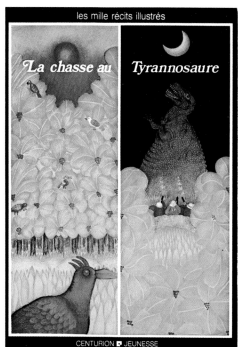

2

3

6

7

8

10

»Hallo, was machst du denn da?«
»Ich wollte schwimmen, aber es ging nicht.«
»Soll ichs dir zeigen?« »O ja.«
»Dann komm zum Flachen. Ich heiße übrigens Harald.«
»Und ich Philip.«

»Ich heiß Inge und will mitmachen.« »Komm zur Kinderschwimmstunde.« »Inge, du kannst schwimmen?« »So'n bißchen.« »Dafür kann Inge nicht fliegen.«

»Das stimmt.« »Kannst du denn fliegen, Harald?« »Nur ein bißchen. Ungefähr einen Meter weit.

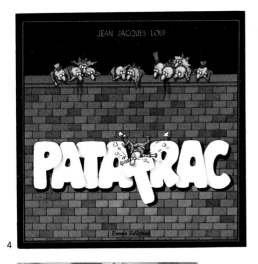

1 Hungary
AD Corvina Verlag
DES Gabriella Hajnal

2 France
AD Centurion Jeunesse
DIR Denys Prache
ILL Tina Mercié

3 Hungary
AD/DES László Reber

4 Italy
AD Emme Edizioni
ILL Jean Jacques Loup

5 Holland
AD Spectrum
ILL David Goddard

6 United States
AD Sauerländer AG
DIR Harlin Quist
ILL Henri Galeron

7 Great Britain
AD Armada Books
ILL Tony Meeuwissen
Children's book

8 Germany
AD Ellermann Verlag
DES Otto Robeck
ILL Anna Robeck
Children's book

9 France
AD Grasset Jeunesse
DIR François Ruy-Vidal
ILL Joëlle Boucher
Children's book

10 Germany
AD Parabel Verlag
ILL Friedrich Karl Waechter

11 Germany
AD Ellermann Verlag
ILL Leo Leonhard
Children's book

12 Italy
AD Emme Edizioni
ILL Guillermo Morillo
Children's book

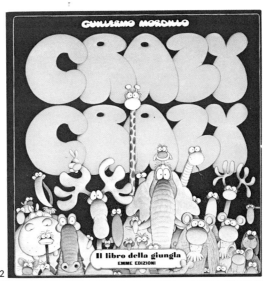

Postage Stamp Designs
Dessins de Timbres-poste
Briefmarken-Entwürfe

1a 1b 2a 2b 3 4 5 6

Universal Postal Union 1874/1974

3½P P&O packet steamer Peninsular 1888

Universal Postal Union 1874/1974

5½P First official airmail Coronation 1911

Universal Postal Union 1874/1974

8P Airmail blue van and postbox 1930

7a-c

2½P JERSEY
Centenary of Universal Postal Union

20P JERSEY
TRANSPORTATION OF MAIL 1974
R.M.S. AQUILA 1874
Centenary of Universal Postal Union

8a-b

30 HELVETIA

30 HELVETIA

9a-b

GHANA 5P

10

POSTES 1,20 RÉPUBLIQUE FRANÇAISE
1874 1974
CENTENAIRE DE L'UNION POSTALE UNIVERSELLE

11

EUROPA CEPT
S 2.50
REPUBLIK ÖSTERREICH

12

UPU
100th. Anniversary of the Universal Postal Union BOTSWANA
3c
Post Office, Palapye, circa 1889

13

UNIVERSAL POSTAL UNION CENTENARY
5k
1874-1974 NIGERIA

14

BƯU CHÍNH 20d
VIỆT NAM CỘNG HÒA

15

ETHIOPIA 15c
U.P.U. CENTENARY 1974

ETHIOPIA 50c
U.P.U. CENTENARY 1974

16a-b

ישראל 0.25
ISRAEL U.P.U. 1874-1974

ISRAEL ישראל
1.30

17a-b

50
DEUTSCHE BUNDESPOST

18

19a-c

1874-1974 40,-
SEABAD UPU CENTENARY
REPUBLIK INDONESIA

1874-1974 65,-
SEABAD UPU CENTENARY
REPUBLIK INDONESIA

1874-1974 100,-
SEABAD UPU CENTENARY
REPUBLIK INDONESIA

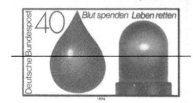
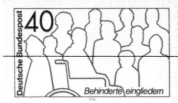

1a

1b

2a

2b

4a-h

6a-f

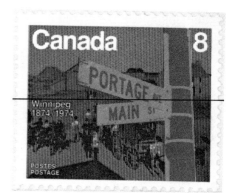

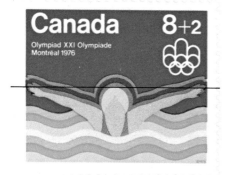

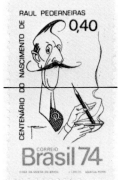

2c

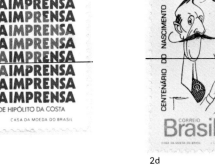

2d

3

1a-b Germany
AD Deutsche Bundespost
DIR/DES Helmut Langer (a)
      Marina Langer-Rosa (b)

2a-d Brazil
AD Ministerio das Comunicaciones
DES Martha Poppe (a)
      J. Carlos (b)

3 Ethiopia
DES Mrs. M. Treska

4a-i Israel
DES A. Kalderon (a, c, g, h)
      O. Adler (b)
      A. Berg (d, e, f)

5a-d Great Britain
AD British Post Office
DIR Stuart Rose
DES Stuart Rose (a)
      Fritz Wegner (b)
      David Gentleman (c)
      Philip Sharland (d)

6a-f Canada
AD Canadian Post Office
DES Stephen Mennie (a, b)
      Jack R. MacDonald (c)
      Wallis & Matanovic (d, e)
      Robert Burns (f)

7a-c Jersey
AD Jersey Post Office
DES Gordon Drummond (a, b)
      Helio Courvoisier (c)

8 France
AD Direction PTT
DES Beat Knoblauch

5a-d

Turner 1775-1851

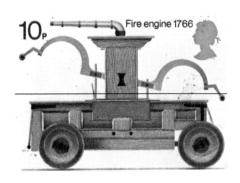

7a

7b

8

7c

1a-e

3a-b

4a-b

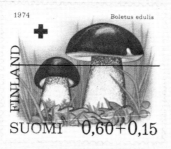

7a-d

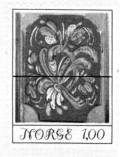

9

10a-c

11a-c

14a-e

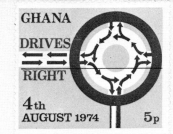

2a-b

2c

5

6a-b

6c-d

1a-e Switzerland
AD Generaldirektion PTT
DES Max Bill (a)
Carl Bruckhardt, Max Bill (b)
Eugen and Max Lenz (c)
Hans Hartmann (c, e)

2a-c Ghana
AG Intergovernmental Philatelic Corp
DES Alexander Larkins

3a-b Bulgaria
AD Ministry of Communications
DES Cyril Gogov

4a-b Republic of Korea
AD Ministry of Communications
DES Mrs Kim, Sung Sil

5 Hungary
AD Ministry of Communications
DES Eva Zombory

6a-d Malta
AD General Post Office
DES Chev. Emvin Cremona

7a-d Finland
AD General Direction of Post and
Telegraphs
DES Paavo Huovinen (a)
Torsten Ekström (b, c)
Pirkko Vahtero (d)

8 New Hebrides Condominium
AD Post and Telecommunications Office
DES J. E. Cooter

9 Austria
AD Ministry of Post
DES Prof. A. Pilch, G. Stefferl

10a-c Norway
DES Chris Dahl (a)
Ottar Helge Johanessen (b, c)

11a-e Brazil
AD Empresa Brasileira de Correios
DES Ary Fagundes (a, b, c, d)
Edvaldo Gato (e)

12 Republic of Botswana
AD Directorate of Post
DES M. F. Bryan

13 Australia
AD Australian Post Office
AG The Doliver Design
DES Ian Dalton

14a-f Belgium
AD Ministry of Posts
DES M. W. Bosschem (a, b, c, d)
M. A. Massonet (e)
M. M. Olyff (f)

8

11d

11e

12

13

14f

Packaging
Emballages
Verpackung

1a-c Germany
AD Zanders Feinpapier GmbH
DES Olaf Leu
Chromolux paper promotion for folding
cartons

1a-b

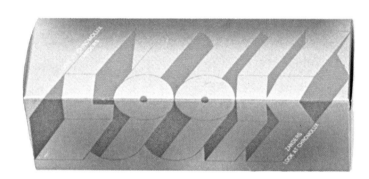

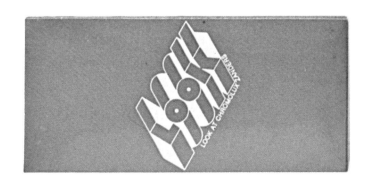

1

2

3

5a-b

6

7

BESSON INSTRUMENTAL

4a

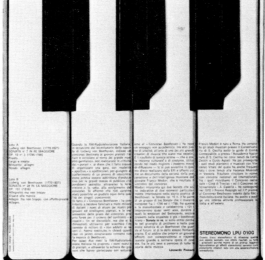

1 Hungary
AD Budavox, Foreign Trade Company
DIR Péterne Zupán
DES Kálmán Molnár
Record sleeve illustrating
telecommunications, Pochette de
disque illustrant les télécommunications,
Schallplattenumschlag, welcher
Telekommunikation illustriert

2 Poland
AD 'Pagart' — Polish Artists' Agency
DES J. R. Olbinski
International song festival programme
cover, Couverture du programme d'un
festival international de la chanson,
Programmumschlag für internationales
Liederfestival

3 Germany
AD Commerzbank
AG Olaf Leu Design
DIR Olaf Leu
DES Olaf Leu, Fritz Hofrichter
ILL Hans Maier

4a-b Italy
AD ERI. Edizioni RAI
DIR/DES Rinaldo Cutini

5a-b Germany
AD/AG Ariola-Eurodisc GmbH
DIR Manfred Vormstein
DES Mouche Vormstein (a)
    Manfred Vormstein (b)
ILL Mouche Vormstein (a)
    Doris Küchler (b)

6 France
AD Production Pérides
AG Pérides
DIR Monique Knichel
DES Barbara Pappé Pougatchoff

7 Germany
AD Deutsche Grammophon
Gesellschaft
DES Dorothea Desmarowitz

8 Great Britain
AD Music for Pleasure Ltd.
AG MFP Design Studio
DIR David Whaim
DES/ILL David Smee
Children's record sleeve, Pochette de
disque pour enfants, Schallplatten-
umschlag für Kinder

9 Great Britain
AD/AG CBS Records
DIR/DES Roslav Szaybo
ILL Don Hunstein

4b

8

9

1

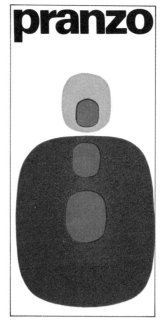

2a

3

2b

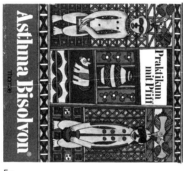

5a

5b

5c-f

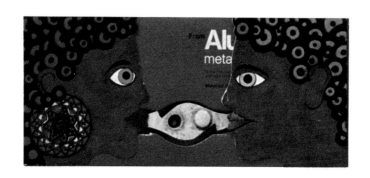

4a-b

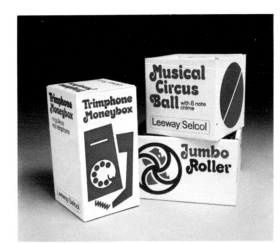

6a-b

1 Italy
AD Bassetti S.p.A.
AG Studio Alfredo Mastellaro
DIR/DES Alfredo Mastellaro
Bed sheets, Draps de lit, Bettwäsche

2a-b Spain
AD Laboratorios Viñas
AG Estudio Moradell
DIR/DES Arcadi Moradell
Pharmaceuticals, Medikamente

3 Holland
AD NVSH (Dutch Ass. for Family
Planning)
AG Nationale Publiciteits
Onderneming BV
DIR/DES Peter Wagner
Condoms, Préservatif

4a-b Germany
AD Eldic
DES Ludvik Feller
Packaging for teaching materials,
Emballage pour matériel d'enseigne-
ment, Verpackung für Lehrmittel

5a-f Germany
AD Thomae Biberach
AG Selinka AG Ravensburg
DIR/DES Friedemann Hett
Asthma Pharmaceuticals

6a-b Great Britain
AD Leeway Selcol
AG Matthew Finch Associates Ltd.
DIR Martin Finch
DES Anthony Hunnybun
ILL Christopher Gillings
Nursery toys, Jouets pour garderie
d'enfants, Spielwaren

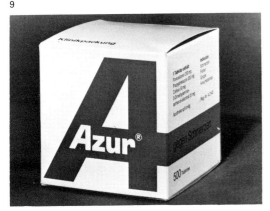

7

Now,
for both aspects of
constipation-
sluggish bowel
and hard dry stools

9

8

7 United States
AD The Purdue Frederick Company
AG Pharmaceuticals Advertising
Associates
DIR Joseph Denaro, David MacInnes
DES Joseph Denaro
ILL G. Kibbee
Laxative

8 United States
AD Denver Chemical Manufacturing
Company
AG Peterson & Blyth Assoc. Inc.
DES John S. Blyth
Throat lozenges, Pastilles pour la gorge,
Halspastillen

9 Germany
AD Steiner Arzneimittel Berlin
DES Erich Unger
Pharmaceuticals, Medikamente

10 United States
AG The Design Partnership Inc.
DIR Bruce Beck
DES Jack Weiss
Autocare product, Produits d'entretien
automobile

10

1

2

4

5

6

8

9

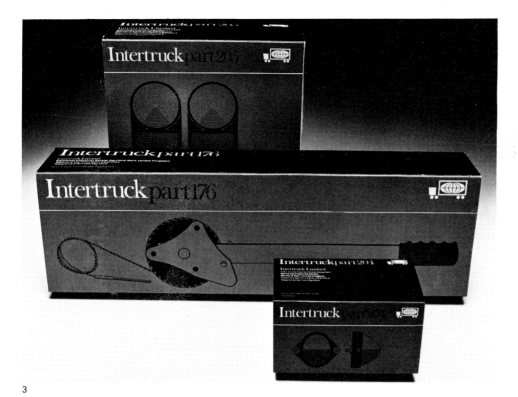

3

7

10

1 Great Britain
AD Thomas Salter Ltd.
AG Allied International Designers
DIR/DES Kevin McGurk
Education toy, Jouet éducatif,
Pädagogische Spielsachen

2 United States
AD Westminster Sports
AG Robert P. Gersin Associates, Inc.
DIR Robert P. Gersin
DES V. Lorenzo Porcelli, Paul Hanson
PHOTO Melabee M. Miller
Table tennis package, Emballage de jeu
de ping-pong, Ping-pong Verpackung

3 Great Britain
AD Intertruck Ltd.
AG Matthew Finch Associates Ltd.
DIR Martin Finch
DES Raymond French
ILL Christopher Gillings
Automotive spares, Pièces automotrices
de rechange, Automotive Ersatzteile

4 Great Britain
AD Thomas Salter Ltd.
AG Allied International Designers
DIR/DES Kevin McGurk
PHOTO Peter Barry
Toys, Jouets, Spielsachen

5 India
AD Bata India Ltd.
AG Bata Studio
DIR/DES Binay Saha
ILL Aloke Guha
Table tennis shoes, Chaussures pour
joueur de ping-pong, Ping-pong Schuhe

6 Great Britain
AD A. Barton & Co. Ltd.
AG Minds Eye Design Consultants
DIR/DES Ray Kyte
Range of packaging, Assortiment
d'emballages, Verpackungssortiment

7 United States
AD Montedison
AG Walter Landor Associates
Paint, Peinture, Farben

8 Spain
AD Valmy
AG Soley Studio
DIR/DES Santiago Soley
Boys' shirts, Chemisier de garçonnet,
Knabenhemden

9 Great Britain
AD Skyline/The Prestige Group
AG Brend Design Associates
Range of household brushes,
Assortiment de brosses pour la maison,
Haushaltsbürsten

10 Great Britain
AD Kenwood Manufacturing Company
AG Pentagram Design Partnership
DIR/DES Mervyn Kurlansky

1

2

4a-b

4c

5

6

3

1 Australia
AD United Distillers Pty. Ltd.
AG George Patterson Pty. Ltd.
DES Cato Hibberd Hawksby Pty. Ltd.
Mixer drinks

2 Great Britain
AD J. Sainsbury Ltd.
AG Sainsbury's Design Studio
DIR/DES Peter J. Dixon
Detergent and soap powder, Lessive et
savon en poudre, Waschmittel

3 Great Britain
AD Suomen Osuuskauppojen
Keskuskunts (SOK)
AG Eurographic Ltd.
Cereals, Céréales, Flocken

4a-c United States
AD Charlotte Charles Inc.
AG Goldsholl Associates
DIR/DES Sheldon Rysner
ILL Parvis Sandigian

5 South Africa
AD Creamline Dairies
AG Jacques Lorraine Crystal
DIR/DES Bruce Backhouse
Yoghurt

6 South Africa
AD Lion Match Co. S.A.
AG Jacques Lorraine Crystal
DIR/DES Tim Errill
Match box, Boîte d'allumettes,
Zündholzschachtel

7 Holland
AD Nestec
AG Form Mediation, International
DIR/DES Pieter Brattinga
ILL Dick Bruna
Children's foods, Nourriture pour
enfants, Esswaren für Kinder

8a-b Great Britain
AD PRIBA – Division of GB-Inno-BM
Belgium
AG Allied International Designers Ltd.
DIR Geoff Gibbons, John Lloyd
Food, Nourriture, Esswaren

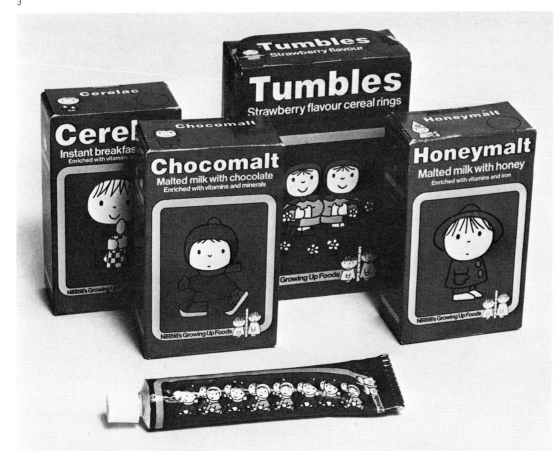

7

8a-b

2

1

4

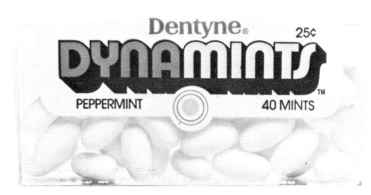

7

8

1 Great Britain
AD The Game Larder
AG Eurographic Ltd.
High quality game birds (farm-reared quail), Gibier de classe (cailles d'élevage), Erstklassige Wildvögel

2 Great Britain
AD The Royal Mint
AG Design Research Unit
DIR/DES June Fraser
Souvenir pack for Decimal coins, Pochette souvenir pour pièces décimales, Souvenirverpackung der Dezimalmünzen

3a-c United States
AD Andrew Jergens Co. (a)
    Vick International (b, c)
AG Peterson & Blyth Assoc. Inc.
DIR John S. Blyth (a)
    Ronald A. Peterson (b, c)
DES Kay Walters (a)
    Ronald A. Peterson (b, c)
Hair shampoo, Shampooing, Haarwaschmittel (a)
Make-up, Maquillage, Schminkmittel (b)
Face wash, Démaquillant, Waschmittel für Gesicht (c)

3a-c

5

4 United States
AD Warner-Lambert Co.
AG Peterson & Blyth Associates Inc.
DIR Ronald A. Peterson
Candy mints, Bonbons à la menthe, Pfefferminzbonbon

5 Italy
AD Industrie Buitoni, Perugina
AG Minale, Tattersfield, Provinciali Ltd.
DIR Marcello Minale, Brian Tattersfield
DES M. Minale, B. Tattersfield, Alex Maranzano

6 Germany
AD Mann & Schröder KG
DES Dieter Zembsch
Toileteries, Toilettenartikel

7 Great Britain
AD Suomen Osuuskauppojen Keskuskunta (SOK)
AG Eurographic Ltd.
Flour, Farine, Mehl

8 Australia
AD Valley Seeds
AG Graphic Folio Pty. Ltd.
DIR/DES Jack Larkin
ILL C. Court
Lawn seed, Semence de gazon, Rasensamen

6

9

10

9 Japan
AD Confectionery français
AG Packaging Direction Co. Ltd.
DIR/DES Katsu Kimura
Confectionery, Confiserie

10 United States
AD Mennen Company
AG Lubalin, Smith, Carnase
DIR/DES Herb Lubalin
Deodorant

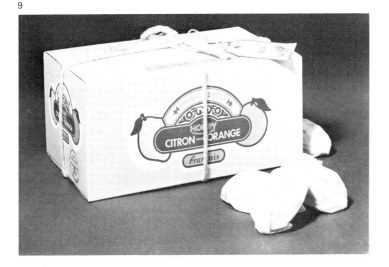

1

2

4

5

6

7

8

9

3

10

11

1 Australia
AD Leo Buring Pty. Ltd.
AG Cato Hibberd Hawksby Pty. Ltd.
Wine casks, Tonneaux de vin,
Weinfässchen

2 Germany
AD Klug & Co KG. Kreuznach
AG/DES Kartonfabrik Annweiler am
Trifels
Winepackaging

3 Great Britain
AD The Ravenhead Company Ltd.
AG Ad Graphics Ltd.
DIR Ken Brown
DES Brian Davis, Bernard Chandler
PHOTO David Lawson
Packaging for mass-produced
glassware, Emballage pour verrerie
de série, Gläserverpackung

4 Great Britain
AD Beecham Foods Ltd.
AG Alan Wagstaff & Partners Ltd.
ILL Jim Hart, Brian Simpson
COPY Henry Latin
Soft drinks, Boissons non-alcoolisées

5 Italy
AD Società Invest
AG Promos srl.
DIR Bob Elliott
DES/ILL Monica Meyer, Marco Negrini
COPY Annamaria Brunner
Wine label, Etiquette de vin

6 Germany
AD Illert KG
DES Karl Heinz Franck
Liqueur label, Etiquette de liqueur

7 Australia
AD Tomasetti & Son Pty. Ltd.
AG Hayes Advertising Pty. Ltd.
DIR/DES Les Mason
ILL Les Mason, Sandie Clark
Wine labels, Etiquettes de vins

8 Australia
AD S. Wynn & Co. Pty. Ltd.
AG Les Mason Graphic Design
DIR/DES Les Mason
ILL Les Mason, Sandie Clark
Rum label, Etiquette de rhum

9 Great Britain
AD ITT Business Systems
AG Matthew Finch Associates Ltd.
DIR/DES Gus Hunnybun
Presentation bottle of malt whisky,
Bouteille échantillon de whisky de malt

10 United States
AD Bacardi Corporation
AG Gianninoto Associates Inc.
DIR John DiGianni
DES A. Accardy
Don Emilio Tequila

11 Great Britain
AD Marks & Spencer Ltd.
AG Pentagram Design Partnership
DIR/DES Alan Fletcher
Vermouth labels, Etiquettes de Vermouth

1

2

3

6

7a

7b

9

8

4

5

7c

7d

10

11

Letraset

1 Mexico
AD Chic-Chic Boutique
AG CoPlan (Comunicación Planificada)
DIR/DES Elena Méndez de la Peña
Boutique

2 Germany
AD Tina-Boutique
AG Procom
DIR Hans Ott
Boutique

3 Hong Kong
AD Department of Overseas Trade,
Australia
AG Graphic Communication Ltd.
DIR/DES Henry Steiner
Shopping bag for Australian Exhibition
in Peking

4 Great Britain
AD Wetherall
AG Negus & Negus
DIR Dick Negus
DES Priscilla Young
Fashion, Modes

5 Great Britain
AD Duffy's Group of Companies
AG Stewart Morrison Harrison Ltd.
DIR John M. Harrison
DES John M. Harrison, Viktoria
Johnson, Ian Morris
Meat and fertiliser producer, Producteur
de viande et d'engrais, Fleisch- und
Düngerproduzent

6 France
AD Brunswick Pro Shop
AG Graphic and Co.
DIR F. Schweblin
DES P. Courivaud
Shopping bags, Sacs à provisions,
Einkaufstaschen

7a-d Sweden
AD A.B. Dalabagerier
AG Lenskog & Co.
DIR/DES Kenneth Bodlund
ILL Rolf Sjödin
Christmas bread packs, Emballages de
pain pour Noël, Weihnachtsverpackung
für Brot

8 Great Britain
AD The General Trading Company
AG National Advertising Corporation
DIR/DES K. Friedeberger
Shopping bags for gift store, Sacs à
provisions pour boutique de cadeaux,
Einkaufstasche für Geschenksboutique

9 Australia
AD Cuisine Doubleday
AG Moffitt and Associates Pty. Ltd.
DIR Valli Moffitt, Kevin Chan
DES Kevin Chan
Shop selling kitchenware, Boutique
vendant des ustensiles de cuisine,
Küchenwarenladen

10 Italy
AD La Mansarda Boutique
DES Rinaldo Cutini
PHOTO Studio Prisma
Ladies' fashion boutique, Boutique de
mode féminine, Modeladen

11 Brazil
AD Letraset do Brasil S.A.
AG Dia Design Ltd.
DIR/DES Gil L. Strunck

Trademarks,
Letterheads,
Co-ordinated design

1a-d Mexico
AD Televisa S.A.
AG Garcia Patto y Asociados
DIR H. Mena
DES Silvio Garcia Patto
Symbol and posters for First World
Communication Encounter, Emblême et
affiches pour la première rencontre
mondiale de la communication, Welt
Kommunikations Konferenz

1a-d

2a-t Argentina
AD Childrens Hospital of Buenos Aires
AG Arq. González Ruiz y Asociados
DIR Guillermo González Ruiz
DES González Ruiz, Ezcurra, Gallo, Solanas
Children's hospital signposting, Panneaux indicateurs dans un hôpital pour enfants, Wegweiser für ein Kinderspital

Lift, Ascenseur (a), Emergency, Secours (b), Enrolment, Inscription, Einschreibung (c), Waiting room, Salle d'attente, Wartesaal (d), Intensive care, Traitements intensifs, Intensivabteilung (e), Pharmacy, Pharmacie, Apotheke (f), Laboratory, Laboratoire, Laboratorium (g), Surgery, Chirurgie, Chirurgie (h), Paediatric clinic, Clinique pédiatrique, Kinderklinik (i), Radiology, Radiologie,

Röntgen (j), Urology, Urologie, Urologie (k), Cardiology, Cardiologie, Kardiologie (l), Infectious diseases, Maladies infectueuses, Infektionskrankheiten (m), Ear/nose/throat, Nez-gorge-oreilles, Hals-Nase und Kehlenkrankheiten (n), First aid, Premiers soins, Erste Hilfe (o), Ophthalmology, Ophtalmologie, Augenabteilung (p) Laundry, Blanchisserie, Wäscherei (q),

Rehabilitation, Centre de réhabilitation (r), Play-room, Salle de jeux, Spielraum (s), Central television (t)

a

b

c

d

e

f

g

h

i

j

k

l

m
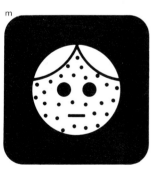

n

o

p

q

r

s

t

1 Great Britain
AD le Yacht-Club de la Méditerranée
DES John Denison-Hunt
Sailing club

7 Bulgaria
DES Stephan Kantscheff
Children's clothing, Kinderkleidung

2 Argentina
AD Tornquist Bank
AG González Ruiz y Asociados
DES Guillermo González Ruiz

8 Great Britain
AD Overseas Computer Consultants
AG Peter Wildbur Associates
DES Peter Wildbur
Computer consultants

3 Spain
AD Delta Express
DES Fernando Medina
Trademark

9 Bulgaria
AD Emil Weltchev
AG Free Practice Bulgaria Union of
Painters
Works of art

4 Finland
AD Kansallis-Osake-Pankki (National
Bank)
DES Heikki Toivola
Bank trademark

10 Austria
AD Otto Jussel KG
AG Vorarlberger Graphik
DIR/DES Othmar Motter
Heating, Sanitäre, Heizungen Klima

5 Canada
AD Colourgraph Reproduction Inc.
AG Chris Yaneff Ltd.
DIR/DES Fred Gotthans
Lithographers

11 Finland
DES Kyösti Varis
AD Neste Oy
Oil processing company

6 Canada
AD Queenswear (Canada) Ltd.
AG Design Collaborative
DIR/DES Rolf Harder
Clothing manufacturer

12 Spain
AD Sofico Vacaciones
AG F. Medina
DIR Guiseppe Lucci
DES Fernando Medina
Travel agency

13 Italy
AD Marcello Masi
DIR/DES Rinaldo Cutini
Office equipment

19 Germany
AD Joseph Janard
DES Klaus Endrikat
Ladies' clothing

14 Bulgaria
AD Plovdiv town puppet show
DES Cyril Gogov
Popular puppet show

20 Czechoslovakia
AD Prefa
AG Propagacni Tvorba
DIR J. Rajlich
DES Ales Vrtal

15 Canada
AD Andex Oil Company Ltd.
AG Supergraphics Design
DIR/DES Michael Pacey
Oil exploration and recovery

21 United States
AD Science Research Associates
AG Edward Hughes Design
DIR/DES Edward Hughes
Student evaluation testing programme

16 United States
AD Brunswick Corp.
AG Goldsholl Associates
DIR Morton Goldsholl
DES Tom Miller
Manufacturing conglomeration

22 Venezuela
AD International Airport Maiquetia
DES Gerd Leufert
Airport

17 United States
AD National Semiconductor Corporation
AG Ken Parkhurst & Associates, Inc.
DIR/DES Ken Parkhurst
Company called 'National' with offices
scattered over the world

23 Great Britain
AD Pochin Ltd.
AG Public Relations Services
DIR/DES Bruce D. Stainsby
Construction company

18 Great Britain
AD Penguin-Longman Books
AG Hans Schleger & Associates
Hard-back children's books

24 United States
AD Spencer Foods Inc.
AG Hoerner Waldorf Corp.
DIR/DES Cyril John Schlosser
Food

1 Great Britain
AD ARDS Shopping Centre
AG Royle/Murgatroyd Design
Association Ltd.
DIR Keith Murgatroyd
DES Anthony D. Forster
Company symbol

7 Mexico
AD Gas Mabarak
AG Dicord
DIR/DES Erick Sherman
Mexico

2 Belgium
AD Machines Collette
DES Paul Ibou
Machinery factory trademark, Estampille
d'une usine de machinerie, Maschinen-
fabrik

8 United States
AD Ciba-Geigy Corporation
AG Ciba-Geigy Corporate Art Services
DIR/DES Stan Baker
Symbol for blood bank, Banque de sang,
Blutbank

3 Germany
AD Stadt Karlsruhe
AG Kunstschule Alsterdamm
DIR Gerd F. Setzke
DES Ricardo Viebranz
City of Karlsruhe

9 Great Britain
AD Weddel Pharmaceuticals Ltd.
AG HDA International
DES Henrion, Cockburn
Pharmaceuticals, Medikamente

4 Italy
AD Unione Commercio e Turismo
AG/DES Mimmo Castellano
Emblem for exhibition, Emblème pour
une exposition

10 Bulgaria
DES Stephan Kantscheff

5 Spain
AD Autopista Enlace S.A.
DES Enric Huguet
Motorway construction, Construction
d'une autoroute, Autobahnkonstruktion

11 United States
AD Children's Research Center
AG/DES Lanny Sommese
Symbol for research center dealing with
children's learning, Centre de recherche
pédagogique, Pädagogisches
Forschungsinstitut

6 Italy
AD Copelli e Bosi
AG/DES Mimmo Castellano

12 United States
AD Franklin Picture Company
AG BBDM, Inc.
DIR/DES Michael Kelly
ILL John Dolby
Picture frame/reproduction firm, Cadre/
usine de reproduction, Bilderrahmen/
Reproduktion

13 Mexico
AD Parlas A.C.
AG Uniseño
DIR/DES Rafael Davidson
ILL Victor M. Gonzalez
Symbol for school for children with
learning disabilities, Ecole d'enfants qui
ont des difficultés à apprendre, Schule
für Kinder, die Lernschwierigkeiten
haben

19 Great Britain
AD Sadler's Wells Theatre
AG Design Research Unit
DIR/DES June Fraser
Symbol for dance companies, Emblème
d'une compagnie de dance, Tanztruppe

14 Great Britain
AD The National Theatre
AG HDA International
DES Henrion, Dennis
Theatre

20 Italy
AD Unione Commercio e Turismo
AG/DES Mimmo Castellano

15 India
AD Directorate of Film Festivals,
Ministry of Information and
Broadcasting
AG NID/HHEC Design Cell
DIR/DES Benoy Sarkar
International film festival

21 Canada
AD Theatre Ontario
AG Chris Yaneff Ltd.
DIR/DES Chris Yaneff
Theatre

16 United States
AD So/California Olympic Committee
AG Robert Miles Runyan & Associates
DIR Robert Miles Runyan
DES James Guerard

22 Spain
AD Sociedad General de Abuas de
Barcelona S.A.
AG/DES Enric Huguet
Water Board, Compagnie des Eaux,
Wasserwerk

17 United States
AD Center Society
AG The Design Partnership
DIR Jack Weiss
DES Fred Miller
Inter-denominational theological
student organization, Organisation
interconfessionnelle d'étudiants en
théologie, Interkonfessionelle Organisa-
tion theologischer Studenten

23 Yugoslavia
AD NT Zurnal
AG Tehnika, Publisher ent.
DIR/DES Ranko Grubac
Journal of science and technology,
Revue de science et de technologie,
Zeitschrift für Wissenschaft und
Technologie

18 Bulgaria
AG Free Practice Bulgaria Union of
Painters
DES Emil Weltchev
Magazine on fish, Revue sur le poisson,
Anglerzeitschrift

24 Australia
AD Film Australia
AG Moffitt and Associates Pty. Ltd.
DIR Valli Moffit, Kevin Chan
DES Kevin Chan
Film corporation

1a

1b

4

5

8a

8b

13

2

3

1a-b Spain
AD UNESA
DES Jose Ros Gonzales
Night clubs, bars, boutiques

2 United States
AD Keepper-Nagen, Inc.
AG The Design Partnership, Inc.
DIR Bruce Beck
DES Adrianne Gregory
Miniwarehouses, Petits entrepôts,
Kleinwarenhäuser

6

7

3 Germany
AD Hi-Fi Studio Ludwig
AG Procom
DIR Hans Ott
Hi-Fi Studio, Studio de haute fidélité

4 Great Britain
AD Beeta Boutique
DES Anthony D. Forster
Boutique

5 Great Britain
AD Lobe
AG Castle Chappell & Partners
DIR/DES Trevor D. Crocker
Radio commercial company, Société de
radio commerciale

9

10

6 Great Britain
AD Boardroom Partnership
AG Lock/Pettersen Ltd.
DIR/DES Tor Pettersen
Paper and board storage unit, Endroit
pour ranger papier et carton

7 Canada
AD Ammo Power Tools
AG Agency Press Ltd.
DIR Don Pullinger
DES Michael Pacey
Power tool rentals, Location d'outils
électriques, Werkzeugvermietung

11

12

8a-b Great Britain
AD Printoli Oy
AG Eurographic Ltd.
Textile printing company, Société
d'imprimerie textile, Textildruck

9 United States
AD Himes Printing Inc.
DES Lanny Sommese
Printer, Imprimerie, Druckerei

10 United States
AD Electronic Technical Corporation
DES Dennis Ichiyama

11 Great Britain
AD The Tanny Group Ltd.
AG Leslie McCombie Associates
DIR Leslie McCombie
DES Martin Elliott
Part of new corporate identity

melonie

14

14 Austria
AD Café Melanie
AG Vorarlberger Graphik
DES Erich Maria Wiener
Café opening, Inauguration d'un café

15 Germany
AD Springer-Verlag New York,
Publishers
DES Peter Klemke
Book series, Série de volumes

16 Great Britain
AD McGillivray
AG HDA International
DES Henrion, Dennis
Insurance agency, Agence d'assurance,
Versicherungs-agentur

12 Great Britain
AD Meubles Format SA
DES John Denison-Hunt
Manufacturer of tubular steel furniture,
Meubles en tubes d'acier,
Stahlrohrmöbel

13 Germany
AD AG Planteam 5, Schweiz
AG Klaus Endrikat, Herbert Wenn
DIR/DES Klaus Endrikat
Architects

15

16

Trademarks,
Letterheads
Marques, en-têtes
Schutzmarken,
Briefköpfe

1 Denmark
AD Goriværk AS
AG Niels Hartmann
Wood protection

2 Germany
AD Evangelische Kirche in Hessen &
Nassau
DES Hans Jürgen Rau
Evangelical church, Evangelische
Kirche

3a-c Great Britain
AD Jet Petrol (UK)
AG Matthew Finch Associates Ltd.
DIR Martin Finch, Raymond French
DES Raymond French, Howard Gerrard
Petrol

4 Denmark
AD AS Phønix
AG Niels Hartmann
Roofing and road building

1

3a-c

Tonbildschau zur Aktion Kirchenwahl

1 (Telefon schellt zweimal)

Sie finden in diesem Prospekt den gesamten Text der Tonbildschau. Die Bilder sind numeriert. Wenn der rote erscheint, nächstes Bild einschalten.

2 Guten Tag, eine Frage bitte, können Sie uns einiges über die geplante Aktion Kirchenwahl sagen? Gern. Da wäre zunächst einmal das auffallende Aktions-symbol.

3 Die Schnecke als dynamischer Blickfang und Illustration unseres Aktions-Mottos.

4 Ein Christ lebt nicht im Schneckenhaus – er wählt und läßt sich wählen. Dieses Motiv eignet sich auch genau so gut für die schwarzweiß Wiedergabe. Wann wird die Wahl stattfinden?

5 Die Wahl der Gemeindevertreter findet am 20. Mai statt. Bis dahin ist noch viel zu planen und vorzubereiten.

6 Wichtig ist, daß es in der ganzen Aktion nicht allein um eine Aktivität für die Wahl geht, sondern auch um eine Aktion für die Kirche. Daran sollten wir bei allen Maßnahmen denken.

7 Hier der Aktionsplan. Er ist in 12 Einzelaktionen eingeteilt. Er erklärt die einzelnen Werbemittel und ihre Einsatzmöglich-keiten und enthält den genauen Terminplan.

8 Sie bekommen den Aktionsplan vorab. Am besten heften Sie ihn an die Wand, dann können Sie jeden einzelnen Schritt verfolgen und die erledigten Maßnahmen abhaken.

9 Es ist sehr wichtig, daß eine solche Aktion gut geplant und sehr genau ausgeführt wird. Deshalb trägt der Aktionsplan auch die Nummer 1. Alle Werbemittel sind so in der Reihen-folge ihres Einsatzes numeriert. Können Sie uns einiges über die einzelnen Maßnahmen sagen?

10 Ja gewiß. Unter Nr. 2 sehen Sie die Gebrauchsanweisung – »Wie wird gewählt«. Kurz und bündig werden alle notwendi-gen Formalitäten den Kirchenwählern erklärt. Wahlberechti-gung, Kandidatenaufstellung, Wahlvorgang usw.

11 Hier der Informationsprospekt »Rechte und Pflichten des Kirchenvorstandes«. Dieser Prospekt wird gezielt an Gemeindemitglieder ausgegeben, die sich für die Kandidatur interessieren.

12 Das Aktionsplakat können Sie in den Formaten A 4 bis A 1 bestellen. Auf dem Plakat ist die jeweilige Gemeinde, an die es geschickt wird, extra eingedruckt. Heften Sie die Plakate an Kirchentüren, ans schwarze Brett von Gemeindehäusern, Schulen oder Jugendheimen.

13 Natürlich auch im Gemeinde-Schaukasten sollte das Plakat hängen. Die Plakataktion sollte erst ab.15. Februar beginnen und in 2 Phasen schwerpunktmäßig verstärkt werden. 1. Phase bis 15. März zum Gewinnen von Wahlvorschlägen. 2. Phase 5.–20. Mai zur Erhöhung der Wahlbeteiligung.

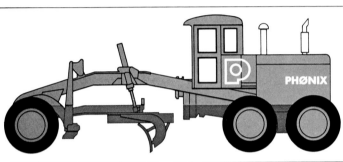
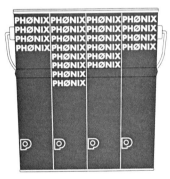

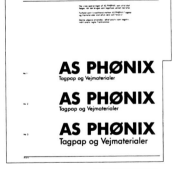

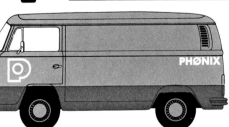
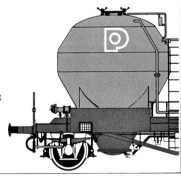
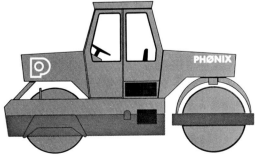

Trademarks,
Letterheads
Marques, en-têtes
Schutzmarken,
Briefköpfe

1 Great Britain
AD The Peterborough & Stamford
Medical Education Committee
AG Design Studio, Publicity Dept.,
Geigy Pharmaceuticals
DIR Brian Stones
DES Ron Stephens
ILL Pete Harrison
Symposium on Rheumatology

2 Denmark
AD Bent Ove Stephensen
AG Walsted & Axelsen Reklamebureau
DES Elisabeth Bandholm

3 Spain
AD/AG Ripoll & Pastor
Self-promotion, Eigenreklame

4 Great Britain
AD Horseshoe Playgroup
AG Cope Design Associates
DIR/DES Peter Cope

5 Great Britain
AD Sue Horne
AG/DES John Marsh
Textile designer's letterhead,
Dessinateur de textiles, Textilient-
werfer

6 Austria
AD Kurt Micheluzzi
AG Atelier Wiener
DES Erich M. Wiener
Writing paper

7 Canada
AD Rob & Heinrichs
AG Burns & Cooper Ltd.
DIR Robert Burns
DES Robert Burns, John Speakman
ILL Rudi Christl
Architect's stationery

8 Great Britain
AD Quixote Productions Ltd.
DIR Dan Parfitt
Corporate Identity for Radio Production
Company

1

2
3

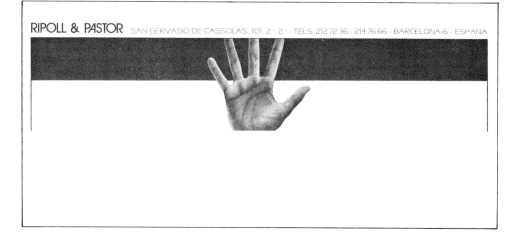

4

Sue Horne Dip AD, Textile Designer.
1 Cornwall Road, Cheam, Surrey, SM2 6DR, England.
Telephone: 01-642 2262.

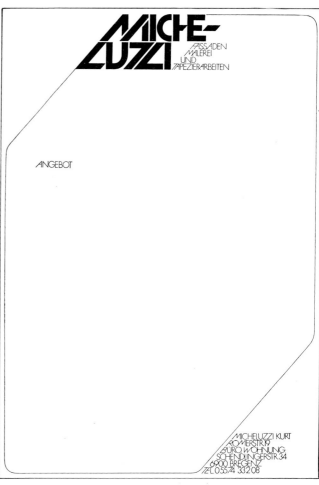

MAICHE-
LUZZI

FASSADEN
MALEREI
UND
TAPEZIERARBEITEN

ANGEBOT

MICHELUZZI KURT
RÖMERSTR 19
BÜRO WOHNUNG
SCHENDLINGERSTR 34
6900 BREGENZ
TEL 05574 33208

5

6

8

7

Robinson and Heinrichs
Architects
819 Yonge Street
Toronto, Ontario
M4W 2G9
(416) 961-5500

Quixote

Quixote Productions Limited, 98 Belsize Lane, Belsize Village, London NW3 5BB.
Tel: 01-794 2424. Directors: Duncan D. Bruce (Managing), Laurence Wolffe.
Registered in England No. 1132813.

Liveware Audio & Lighting Hire Ltd.
Trident House, St. Anne's Court, London W1V 3AW Tel: 01-734 9901/6
Rehearsal Theatre, 1B Bond Street, Ealing W5.
Registered office, 36 Brewer Street W1. Registration No. 1195532

Directors: Bob Hill Simon Friend

Trebor Sharps'
National Sales Conference
1974

1 2

3

Film Producers   6/91 Muston Street
Manufacturers and   Mosman
Operators of Coin   New South Wales 2088
Operated Movie
Viewers   Telephone 969 8820

4

"études et réalisations photographiques"
ATV à 10 avenue Spinoza, Ivry 94200 ☎ 670 01 54

5

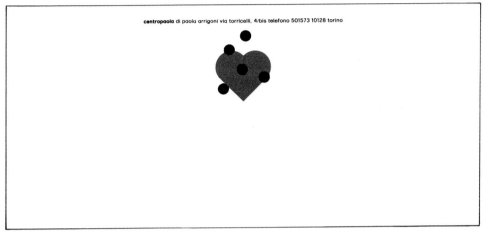

6

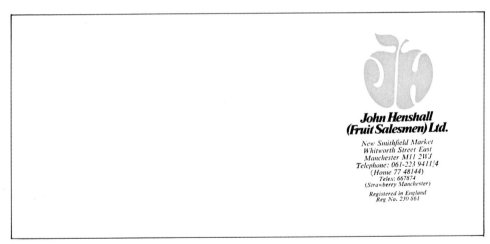

7

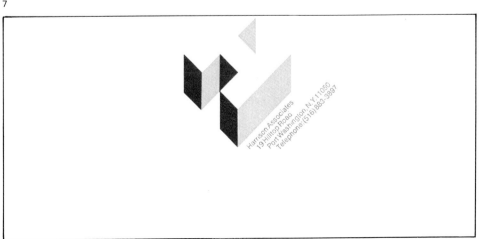

8

1
AD Bob Hill, Liveware
AG Vernon Oakley Design Ltd.
DIR/DES Ken Scott
ILL Mike Farrell

2 Great Britain
AD Trebor Sharps
AG Norman Boyd Design Ltd.
DIR Terence Wilson
DES Lynn North
Letterhead and invitation for national
sales conference, Invitation pour une
conférence nationale de ventes,
Einladung für eine nationale
Verkaufskonferenz

3 Australia
AD Keyhole Moving Picture Company
Pty. Ltd.
AG Cato Hibberd Hawksby Ltd.
Letterhead for film producers,
Producteurs de films, Filmproduzenten

4 France
AD ATV
AG Grapus

5 Great Britain
AD Rosemary Dunnage & Associates
AG Bruce D. Stainsby Graphic Design
Letterhead for public relations and
communications company, Société de
relation publique et de communications,
Reklame- und Kommunikationsfirma

6 Italy
AD Centro Paola
AG Giob
DIR/DES R. Del Sordo

7 Great Britain
AD John Henshall
AG Derwent Design
DES William Porter

8 United States
AD/AG Harrison Ass.
DIR/DES Peter Harrison

1 Great Britain
AD Standplan Ltd.
AG Minale, Tattersfield, Provinciali Ltd.
DIR/DES Marcello Minale, Brian
Tattersfield
COPY B. Tattersfield

2 Great Britain
AD Leeds Judean Youth Club
AG De Morgan Associates
DIR/DES Jonathan de Morgan
Jewish youth club, Club de jeunesse
juive, Jüdischer Jugendklub

3 Denmark
AD/AG Weber & Sorensen A/S
DIR Frits Møller
DES Biswajit Ganguli

4 Germany
AD/DES Ludvig Feller
Personal letterhead

5 Canada
AD Peter Shewchuk Sound
AG Geoff Cross/Design
DIR/DES Geoff Cross
Film sound recording, Enregistrement
du son d'un film, Tonaufnahmen für Film

6 United States
AD Anthony Lent
DES Joseph S. Scorsone
Letterhead for medieval-style jeweller,
Joailler de style médiéval, Juwelier im
mittelalterlichen Stil

7 Great Britain
AD Royal Northern College of Music
AG Royle/Murgatroyd Design Ass. Ltd.
DIR/DES Keith Murgatroyd

8 Italy
AD Nino Lo Duca
DES Angelo Sganzerla

JUMBO CONTRACTS Standplan, 32 Paddington Street, London W1M 3RG, Tel. 01-935 8802

1

Leeds   Judean Youth Club

Samuel Henry Lyons Youth Centre
420 Street Lane
Leeds LS17 6RL
Telephone Leeds 681730

Affiliated to the
National Association of Youth Clubs
National Association of Boys Clubs
Association for Jewish Youth

Secretary
Mrs J Heptonstall
Telephone Leeds 656149

Presidents
L E Wigoder MA BDS JP
B Lyons CBE JP

2

weber & sørensen
reklamebureau a/s
sct clemenstorv 8. 8000 århus c
telefon (06) 12 70 77

3

4

Ludvik Feller
Graphic designer
CSVU AIGA ICOGRADA

Nonverbal communication
Staatliche Hochschule
für bildende Künste

1000 Berlin 61
Großbeerenstraße 49
Tel.: 7857425

Berliner
Disconto Bank
324/1544

Peter Shewchuk Sound
31 Playter Crescent
Toronto 355, Ontario
Phone 465 5975

PSS

5

6

*Royal
Northern College
of Music*

Patron : Her Majesty The Queen / President : Her Royal Highness The Duchess of Kent

From the Principal

124 Oxford Road, Manchester M13 9RD / Telephone 061 273 6283

8

NLD

Nino Lo Duca fotografo
st. 20100 Milano via Gesù 8 telefono 781385
ab. 20136 Milano v.le Bligny 44 telefono 585309

Warehouse: 611 West 129 Street New York, New York 10027 Telephone (212) 866-6052

Administration: c/o Theatre Development Fund 1564 Broadway New York, New York 10036 Telephone (212) 757-4883

A project of Theatre Development Fund, a non-profit organization

1

2

3

4

LORD JOHN

Lord John Limited
1 Cowley Road
The Vale
Acton London W3 7YD
Telephone 01-749 1395

Stuart Kendall

Member of the Raybeck Group of Companies
Directors B Raven M Sugarman I Kaffel ACA A Bergson M Gerold L Sinclair R Woolsgrove
Registered office 309 Oxford Street W1R 2LE Registered no 248207 London

John Martin and Artists Limited
Artists' Agents
5 Wardour Street London W1V 3HE Telephone 01-734 9000
Directors: W.Bowen-Davies C.M.Bowen-Davies L.L.Kemp

5

48 Chandos Street St Leonards
New South Wales 2065
Telephone 43 4123/4 432109

Office also at Canberra ACT

Eric A Towell FRAIA ARIBA
Eve Laron ARAIA ARIBA

Eric Towell & Partners Pty Ltd / Architects

6

1061 Wien, Gumpendorfer Straße 83, Postfach 465, Telefon 57 57 62, 57 63 62, 57 51 73

VERSICHERUNG FÜR DIE BAUWIRTSCHAFT

Aktiengesellschaft

Bauwesen-
Haftpflicht-
Unfall-
Rechtschutz-
und Kfz.-
Versicherung

Bankverbindungen: Österreichische Länderbank 109-111-609/00 – Postsparkasse 2368.290 – Volksbank Landstraße 36890

7   8

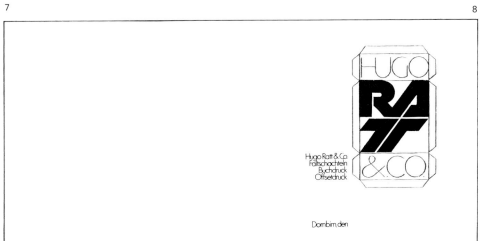

Hugo Ratt & Co
Faltschachteln
Buchdruck
Offsetdruck

Dornbirn,den

1 Great Britain
AD Sam Bellingham
DES David Tyrell
Stationery for photographer's agent,
Fourniture pour agence de photographe,
Schreibwaren für einen Photographen-
agentur

2 United States
AD Theatre Development Fund
AG Charles Fuhrman and Edith Allgood
DIR/DES Charles Fuhrman
ILL Edith Allgood
Direct mail brochure announcing
costume collection programme,
Brochure postées annonçant le
programme d'une collection de
costumes, Postversandbroschüre über
ein Programm einer Kostümausstellung

3 Great Britain
AD Lord John
AG John Harris Design Assoc.
DIR John Harris
DES Peter Kerr

4 Great Britain
AD/AG Stuart Kendall

5 Great Britain
AD John Martin and Artists Ltd.
DES Roger Harris

6 Australia
AD Eric Towell & Partners
AG Nielsen Design Associates Pty. Ltd.
DIR/DES John Spatchurst

7 Austria
AD Versicherung für die Bauwirtschaft
AG Watzlwerk
DIR/DES Peter Watzl

8 Austria
AD Ratt
AG Atelier Wiener
DES Erich M. Wiener

Screen advertising,
Titles
Annonces de l'écran,
Titres
Film- und TV-Werbung,Titel

1 Canada
AD National Film Board of Canada
DES Ryan Larkin

2a-b Canada
AD Canadian Broadcasting Corporation
AG Burton Kramer Associates Ltd.
DIR/DES Burton Kramer, Allan Fleming
ILL Vladimir Goetzelman
Television

2a

2b

1

2

4

5

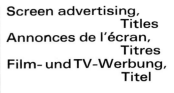

Screen advertising,
Titles
Annonces de l'écran,
Titres
Film- und TV-Werbung,
Titel

1 Holland
AD Verkoopmaatschappij Zanussi BV . .
AG Nationale Publiciteits
Onderneming BV
TV DIR Erik de Vries, Toon Broeksma
DES Danylo Ducak
Washing machine

2 Holland
AD Clin-Midy
AG Nationale Publiciteits
Onderneming BV
DIR Peter Wagner
TV DIR Toon Broeksma
Anti-flu pharmaceutical, Medikamente

3 Italy
AD Olivetti, S.A.
DES Ornella Linke-Bossi
Audiovisual aid training for electronic
calculators

4 Holland
AD Bristol Myers
AG Nationale Publiciteits
Onderneming BV
DIR Peter Wagner
ANIMATION Kaj Pindale
ILL Rowland B. Wilson
Deodorants

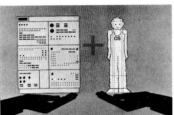

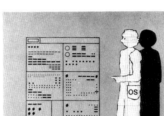

5 Great Britain
AD Cadbury/Schweppes 'Brobat Bloo'
AG PLN Partners
DIR Russell Hall
DES Gray Jolliffe
COPY Roger Nokes
Household product

6 Switzerland
AD Schweizer Fernsehen
AG Charlotte and Remo Guidi
DIR Charlotte Guidi
ILL Remo Guidi
TV titles for breaks in sports-results
programme

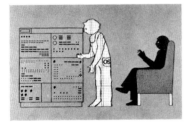
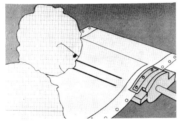

3

6

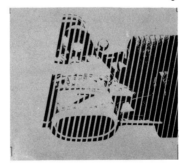

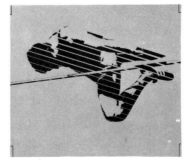

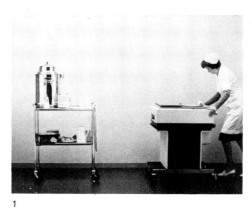
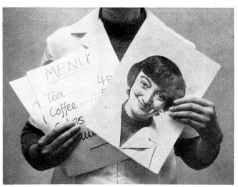

1

2

3a

3b

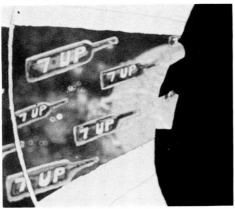

4

5

Screen advertising, Titles
Annonces de l'écran, Titres
Film- und TV-Werbung, Titel

1 Great Britain
AD Rank Xerox Ltd.
AG Young & Rubicam Ltd.
DIR M. Stephenson
PRODUCTION CO. Moving Picture Co.
COPY G. Cadwallader
Photostat machine, Kopiermaschine

2 Great Britain
AD H. J. Heinz Co. Ltd.
AG Young & Rubicam Ltd.
DIR D. Simons
PRODUCTION CO. R.S.A.
COPY J. Clarke
Soup, Potage, Suppen

3a-b Argentina
AD Colchones Ideal S.A. (a)
       Aereolineas Argentinas (b)
AG Garcia Patto y Asociados
DES Silvio Garcia Patto
ILL Cine Creativo S.A.
Mattresses, Matelas, Matratze (a)
Airline (b)

4 Holland
AD Seven-Up Nederland B.V.
AG Prad B.V.
ANIMATION/ART Harold F. Mack
PRODUCTION CO. Anglo Dutch Group
Soft drink, Boissons non-alcoolisées,
Alkoholfreie Getränke

5 Holland
AD Het Nederlands Zuivelbureau
AG Prad B.V.
CONCEPT Paul Mertz, Michiel
Beishuizen
PRODUCTION CO. Bussmann &
Llewellyn
Milk, Lait

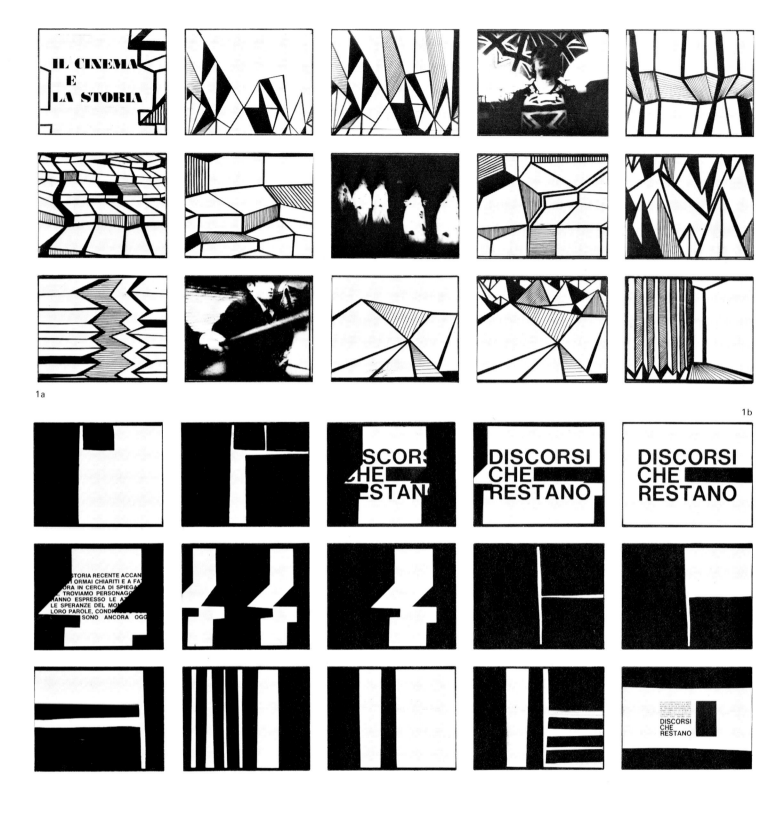

1a

1b

3

Screen advertising,
Titles
Annonces de l'écran,
Titres
Film- und TV-Werbung,
Titel

1a-b Italy
AD RAI — Radiotelevisione Italiana
AG Studio Ruffolo
DIR/DES Sergio Ruffolo
Cultural Programmes

2a Great Britain
AD Lyons Four Seasons Salads
AG McCann Erickson, London
STUDIO Wyatt-Cattaneo Ltd.
PROD/DES Tony Cattaneo

2b Great Britain
AD Golden Wonder Crisps
AG Masius Wynne Williams
STUDIO Wyatt-Cattaneo Ltd.
PROD/DES Ron Wyatt

2c Great Britain
AD Lyons Tetley Tea Bags
AG McCann Erickson, London
STUDIO Wyatt-Cattaneo Ltd.
PROD/DES Tony Cattaneo

2d Great Britain
AD Wyatt-Cattaneo Ltd.
PROD/DES Alison De Vere
Café Bar, entertainment film

3 Great Britain
AD/AG Granada Television
ILL Anna Farrar
Children's Programme

2a

2b

2c

2d

144-145

1

3

pysy
terveenä

2

4

SEE YOUR TRAVEL AGENT
OR FILL IN THE COUPON IN TV TIMES

Screen advertising,
Titles
Annonces de l'écran,
Titres
Film- und TV-Werbung,
Titel

1 Germany
AD Saarländischer Rundfunk Fernsehen
DES Prof. G. H. Magnus
TV programme on 17th–20th-Century
light literature, Programme de télévision
sur la littérature légère, du 17ème–
20ème siècles, Trivialliteratur des
17.–20. Jahrhunderts

2 Finland
AD The Finnish Broadcasting Co.
AG The Finnish Broadcasting Company
TV 1
DIR/DES Tapio Soivio
PHOTO Aarre Aalto, Raimo Hiltunen
TV programmes on health services,
Programme de télévision sur les services
de santé, Fernsehprogramme über das
Gesundheitsservice

3 Great Britain
AD Look-In magazine
AG Greendow Commercials
DIR Peter Clark, Mick Monaghan
DES Mick Monaghan
Children's TV comic

4 Great Britain
AD Wallace Arnold
AG L.A.M. (Manchester)
DIR Michel Huet
DES Peter Beard
ANIMATION Roy Evans
Travel agent, Agence de voyage,
Reisebureau

1a

1b

2c

2d

2e

Screen advertising,
Titles
Annonces de l'écran,
Titres
Film- und TV-Werbung,
Titel

2a-b

3

1a-b Great Britain
AD BBC TV
PRODUCER Roy Tipping
DIR/DES Michael Graham-Smith
ILL Pauline Ellison
TV performance of 'Carmina Burana',
Représentation télévisée de 'Carmina
Burana', Fernsehvorstellung der
'Carmina Burana'

2a-e Great Britain
AD BBC TV
DIR Colin Cheesman
DES Ian Hewitt (a, b)
    Bernard Lodge (c, e)
    Pauline Talbot (d)
TV title sequences, Génériques de films
à la télévision, Fernsehvorspann

3 Ireland
AD/AG Radio Telefis Eireann Design
Studio
ILL Jan Mitchell
TV children's stories, Histoires pour
enfants à la télévision,
Fernsehgeschichten für Kinder

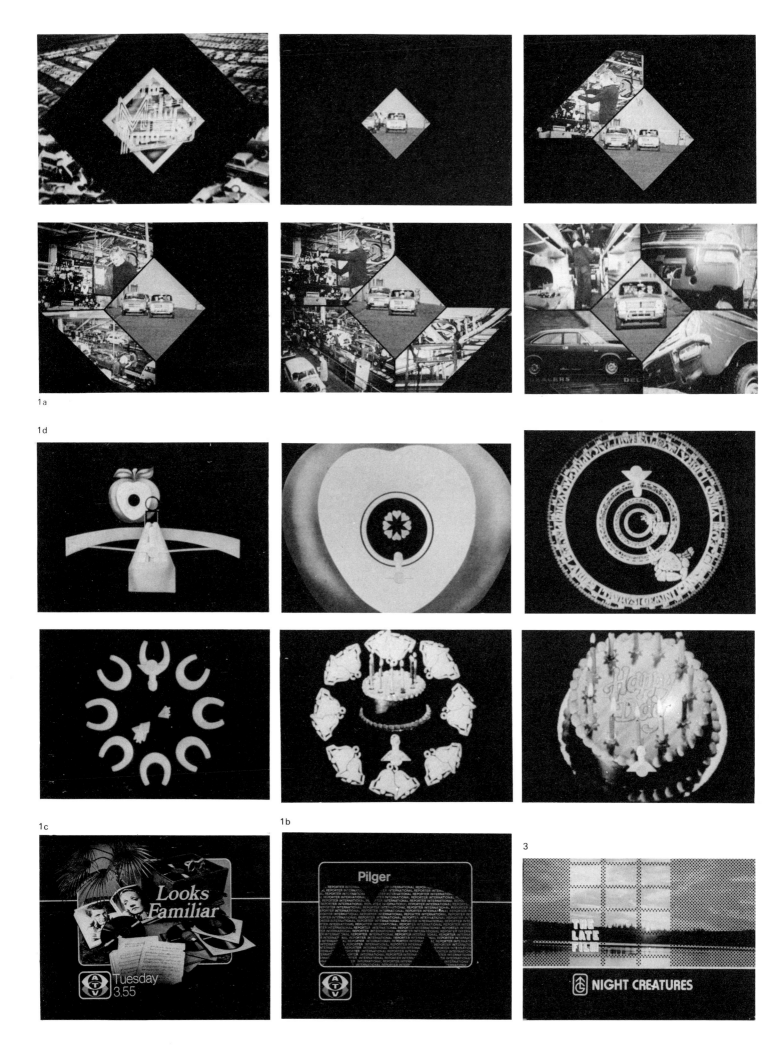

1a

1d

1c

1b

3

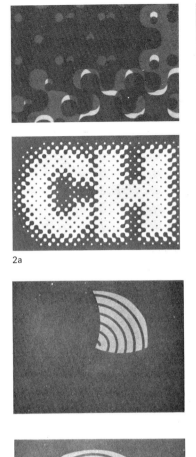

2a

Screen advertising,
Titles
Annonces de l'écran,
Titres
Film- und TV-Werbung,
Titel

1a-d Great Britain
AD ATV Network Ltd.
AG Graphic Design Studio, ATV Centre
DIR Geoff Pearson (a)
    Mike Shaw (b)
    Steve Safe (c, d)
DES Geoff Pearson, Mike Shaw (a)
    Mike Shaw (b)
    Steve Safe (c, d)
Documentary on the British motor
industry (a), Audience participation
light-entertainment show (b), Nostalgia
programme on looking back at 1930's
etc. (c), Documentary series (d)

2a-b Switzerland
AD/AG Schweizer Fernsehen
DIR Charlotte Guidi
DES Bernard Rohner (a)
    Jürg Grüniger (b)
Magazine (a), News (b)

3 Great Britain
AD Granada Television
AG Graphic Design Dept.
DES Philip Buckley
Title for film on TV

4a-b Great Britain
AD Granada TV
DIR/DES Jim Quick
Weather slides

2b

4a-b

Direct Mail,
Company reports,
House organs

Brochures,
Rapports annuels,
Journaux d'entreprises

Broschüren,
Jahresberichte,
Hauszeitschriften

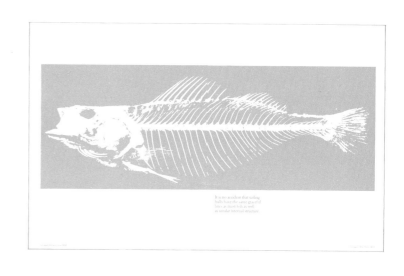

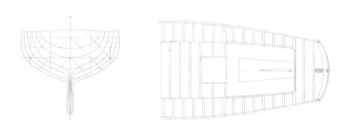

1a–c

Keels, like dorsal and ventral
fins, prevent lateral motion
and control direction–as well
as keeping the boat upright,
of course. Rudders turn boats
in precisely the same way as
fish use their fins and tails to
change direction underwater.

Georgian Offset Matte 140M

Georgian Offset Matte 140M

1a-c Canada
AD Abitibi
AG Burns & Cooper Ltd.
DIR Robert Burns
DES Robert Burns, John Speakman
ILL Tim Saunders
Promotion for coated paper, Papier
couché, Lackiertes Papier

2a-c Canada
AD MAI Canada
AG Burns & Cooper Ltd.
DIR/DES Robert Burns
ILL Heather Cooper, Dawn Tennant
Booklet on compact computer system

3 Canada
AD Abitibi
AG Burns & Cooper Ltd.
DIR Robert Burns
DES Robert Burns, John Speakman,
Heather Cooper
Promotion kit for Bond paper, Trousseau
de promotion pour du papier Bond,
Reklamemappe für Bond Papier

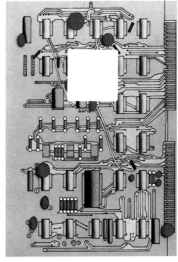

2a-c

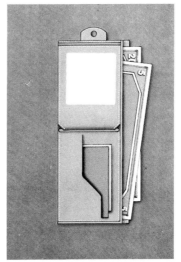

3

DR. NOST
HAY FEV

THE N
TRA
BENE

THE EQUITABLE
MAGNETIC
MATRIMONIAL
AGENCY

ABITIBI PROVINCIAL PAPER

This Company showed exceptional imagination in applying modern technology
to traditional social problems. The significance of magnetism in marriage was
but dimly appreciated until Equitable's ads appeared, explaining that only
through its patented process could one be certain of avoiding what it called the
"horrors of anti-magnetic marriage." Using an extraordinary elaborate apparatus,
the Company tested the magnetic field surrounding each marital candidate,
and refused to recommend marriage for those who showed opposite polarity,
wandering polarity, no polarity, or glimm'ning of the gizzard. This last is a
disorder found only in those possessing an extremely high degree of animal
magnetism. The corporate motto was "Magnetic Attraction Guarantees Satisfaction."

The characteristics of early bond paper are still present today in Abitibi's
Provincial Bond, the ideal all-purpose bond for every stationery and business form
requirement, as well as for a host of other uses. It is available in white and

PROVINCIAL BOND

THE IDEAL NO.7 BOND

PINK

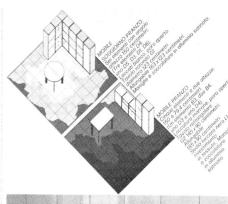

1a-e

Nelle
librerie a cristalleria
possono essere inseriti cassetti
interni a vista in betulla naturale.
Nell'interno
dei cassetti può essere sistemato
un sapiente gioco in legno ad incastri
Così il vano del cassetto diventa ben diviso in tanti utili spazi.
Le piccole
e comode maniglie sono
in metallo cromato. Così pure
il profilo dei piani dei mobili e le finiture dei tavoli

Un piano
superiore a sbalzo,
di leggero spessore,
robusto, aereo
è una caratteristica
molto importante
del design
della serie S19.

4c-d

la prima cucina interamente in legno

SCHIFFINI

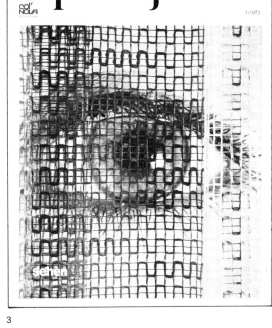

Direct Mail
Brochures
Broschüren

1a-e Italy
AD Sorgente dei Mobili
AG Studioelle
DIR Ennio Lucini
DES Giampietro Ceretti
PHOTO Antonini Studio 17,
        Aldo Ballo (a, b)
        A. Gui (c, d, e)
COPY Ennio Lucini
Catalogue, Katalog

2 Great Britain
AD Airfix Plastics Ltd.
AG Conran Associates
DIR/DES John White
ILL Chris Thomson
COPY Richard Gordon-Freeman
Crayonne door-numbers, Numéros de
portes, Crayonne Hausnummern

3 Germany
AD Enka Glanzstoff
AG Stankowski & Partners
DIR Anton Stankowski
DES Karl Duschek
ILL Dr. Fink
Textiles

4a-d Italy
AD Schiffini
AG Studioelle
DIR Ennio Lucini
DES Giampietro Ceretti
PHOTO Antonini, Studio 17
COPY Ennio Lucini

5 Yugoslavia
AD Belgrade International Theatre
Festival
AG Studio Structure
DIR Slobodan Masic
DES Saveta Masic, Slobodan Masic

6 Switzerland
AD ISAL-Gruppe
AG Atelier Zeugin AGI/ASG/BSR
DIR/DES Mark Zeugin
Windows and Façades, Fenêtres et
façades, Fernstern und Fassaden

2

3

4a-b

5

6

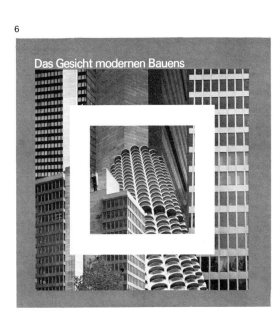

1a-c

3

4

7

6b

6c

6a

8a-b

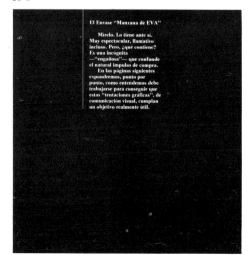

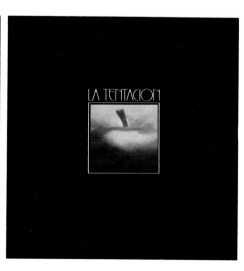

2a-b

5

CHAIRS IN PARIS OUT OF TOWN

9

No.1 Charlotte Square

is typical of the best of that unique combination of town planning and distinguished architecture—the New Town. Its elegant streets, graceful crescents and spacious squares form a national treasure of the first importance, of which that great French authority M. François Sorlin has written "It has no equivalent anywhere in the world".

Even in such surroundings Charlotte Square is outstanding. Sir John Summerson has described it as "the first architectural triumph of the New Edinburgh". Sir Basil Spence has written "Here

we find civic architecture at its best, created by a master".

Architects and planners from every corner of the globe visit the New Town as on a pilgrimage. Its conservation is one of the subjects on which world attention will be focussed during European Architectural Heritage Year.

Yet Scotland in general, and Edinburgh in particular, lack any focal point for the world wide interest generated by this priceless heritage—a house appropriately furnished and open to public view, whose interior reflects the life-style of those who built the New Town, and which tells the story of its grand design.

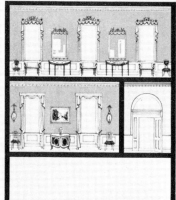

No.1 Charlotte Square, Edinburgh

1a–b

4

Boat Fleet

Thames Motor Boat Company Limited

is miles more fun. The passing scene up n Court or down river ds extra interest to rty Boats provide good or wedding lunches, ail parties and, if you discos for dancing. on board every vessel ficiently organised.

The fleet of Party Boats is available for evening or day hire for 8 or 4 hours, up river or down river from Westminster and other piers. (More about this on the river card). Party Boats vary in size from the 106 feet of the m.v. Connaught to the 63 feet of the m.v. Princess Freda. Detailed facts about each vessel are on the cards that follow. Party Boats are operated by

Thames Motor Boat Company who have considerable experience arranging every kind of passenger boat activity on London's river.

Choose a Party Boat for your next function whether it be a matter of business, a club outing or some more private happening.
Photographs by courtesy of the British Tourist Authority

6

7a–b

The Jesus File

A resource pack of illustrated scripture selections, posters, and guide sheets taken from Good News told by John in Today's English Version

Invaluable for scripture-centred activities in youth, young adult and student groups, residential conferences, evangelistic projects and as RE resource material.

It can be used as the basis for group work and as a launch-pad for a 'communication project'

| John 3.1–21 |
| John 4.5 30 30 12 |
| John 9.1–41 |
| John 10.7–21 |
| John 6.35 |
| John 12.24–25 |
| John 18.37–38 |

Humana:
Dedicated to
Quality
Health Care

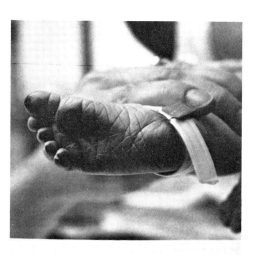

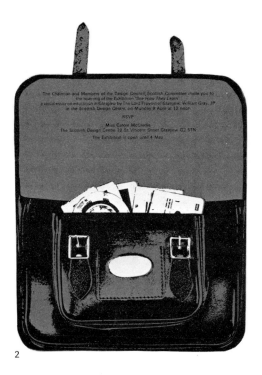

2

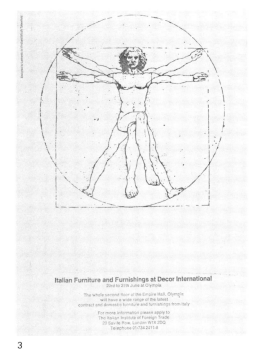

Italian Furniture and Furnishings at Decor International

23rd to 27th June at Olympia

The whole second floor of the Empire Hall, Olympia
will have a wide range of the latest
contract and domestic furniture and furnishings from Italy

For more information please apply to
The Italian Institute of Foreign Trade
20 Savile Row, London W1X 2DQ
Telephone 01-734 2411-8

3

5a

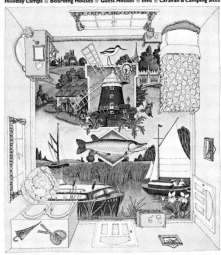

5b

8

1a-b Great Britain
AD The National Trust for Scotland
AG Forth Studios Ltd.
DIR John Martin
DES Dorothy Steedman
ILL James Gorman, John Martin
Restoration of a Georgian house,
Restauration d'une demeure géorgienne,
Restaurierung eines alten Hauses

2 Great Britain
AD Scottish Design Centre
AG Quad Graphic Design
DIR David Watson, Gordon Rennie
DES Ian McIlroy
Invitation card for exhibition, Carte
d'invitation à une exposition,
Einladung zu einer Ausstellung

3 Italy
AD Italian Institute of Foreign Trade
AG Minale, Tattersfield, Provinciali Ltd.
DIR/DES Marcello Minale, Brian
Tattersfield
COPY Brian Tattersfield
Italian furniture exhibition, Exposition
de meubles italiens, Ausstellung
italienischer Möbel

4 Great Britain
AD Thames Motor Boat Co.
AG Trickett & Webb Ltd.
DIR Lynn Trickett, Brian Webb
DES Lynn Trickett, Brian Webb, Colin
Sands
Boat company, Compagnie navale,
Schiffsfirma

5a-b Great Britain
AD English Tourist Board
AG Derek Forsyth Graphics Ltd.
DIR Derek Forsyth
DES Paul Sewell
ILL Head Office
Tourism

6 Great Britain
AD British and Foreign Bible Society
AG Barry Dunnage
DES/PHOTO Barry Dunnage
ILL Rachel Beckingham
Study material based on St John's
gospel, Matériau d'étude basé sur
l'Evangile de Saint Jean, Studienmaterial
über das Johannesevangelium

7a-b United States
AD Humana Inc.
AG Lippincott & Margulies Inc.
DIR/DES Frank Deleno
ILL Bruce Davidson

8 Great Britain
AD Habitat
AG Conran Associates
DIR/DES Peter Templeman
ILL Ray Ogden
Guide to 30 of London's best restaurants,
Guide des 30 meilleurs restaurants de
Londres, Handbuch über die 30 besten
Restaurante in London

1a-b

3a-d

2a-b

Introduction

Main Meals

Lancashire Hot Pot
Serves: 4 *illustrated on cover*
Cooking time: 2 hours
Oven temperature: 350°F
Mark 4

1¼ lb middle neck of mutton, cut
  into chops
2 lamb's kidneys, skinned, cored and
  sliced
1 large onion, peeled and sliced
1 lb potatoes, peeled and thickly
  sliced
1 teaspoonful curry powder
salt and pepper
¾ pint stock

Method
Place the chops in the bottom of
a casserole. Cover with a layer
of kidneys and onions. Season
with salt, pepper and curry
powder.

Pour over the stock and arrange
potatoes slightly overlapping on
top.

Cover and bake for 2 hours until
meat is tender. Remove lid for
last 25 minutes of cooking time

to brown the potatoes.

Serve hot with red cabbage.

**Crispy Cheese and Tomato
Cod Cutlets**
Serves: 4 *illustrated on page 50*
Cooking time: 25-30 minutes
Oven temperature: 375°F
Mark 5

4 cod cutlets
salt and pepper
1 x 14 oz can tomatoes
4 oz fresh white breadcrumbs
4 oz grated cheese

Method
Place cod cutlets in an
ovenproof dish and season with
salt and pepper. Pour over
tomatoes.

Mix together breadcrumbs and
cheese and sprinkle over the top.

Bake for 25-30 minutes until
topping is golden.

Serve hot.

6
31

1a-b Germany
AD Burda Verlag GmbH
AG Apollon
DIR/DES Lutz Roeder
COPY Nanna Michael
Media promotion

2a-b Great Britain
AD Atora (R.H.M. Foods Ltd.)
AG Cato, Johnson Associates
DIR/DES Ginger Tilley
PHOTO John Lee
ILL Roger Harris, Glynn West, Ginger
Tilley
Cook book for suet, Livre de recettes
pour la graisse de bœuf, Kochbuch über
den Gebrauch von Talg

3a-d Great Britain
AD Goldenlay Eggs
AG Stillwell/Stillwell
DIR Peter Stillwell
DES Ginger Tilley
Eggs, Oeufs, Eier

4a-b Sweden
AD AB Dalabagerier
AG Lenskog & Co.
DIR/DES Kenneth Bodlund
ILL Dag Sundberg
COPY Steve Trygg
Bread, Pain, Brot

4a-b

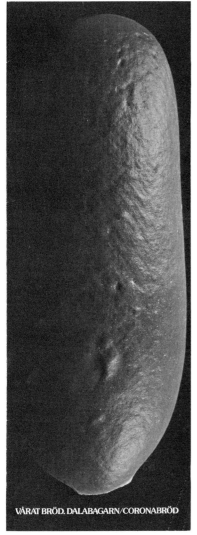

VÅRAT BRÖD, DALABAGARN/CORONABRÖD

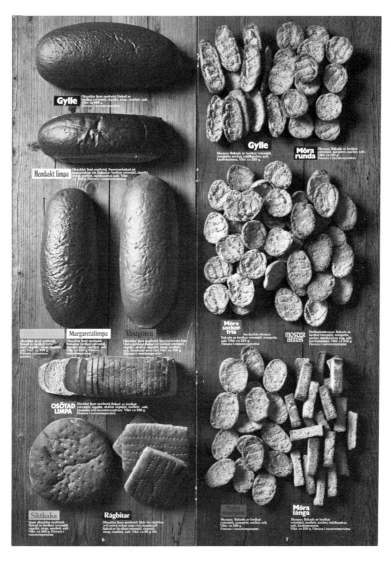

1

For food advertisers: a vital ingredient in any well-balanced diet.

2

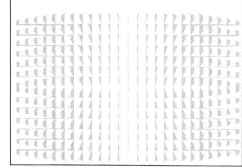

FINANCIAL TIMES
INDUSTRIAL ARCHITECTURE
AWARD 1974

3a

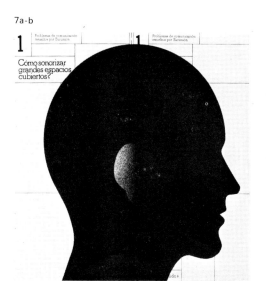

Wir kämpfen für Ihr Produkt, als wäre es unser eigenes.

Wir Comptoniken.

5a-b

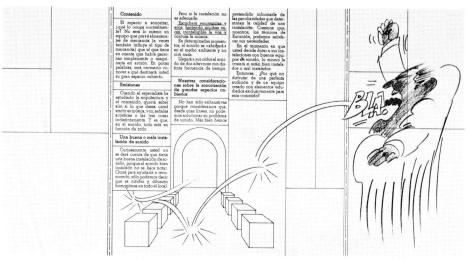

Die Höschenwindel Pampers ist offensichtlich allen Windelsystemen überlegen. Und was hat unsere Werbung daraus gemacht?

Eine kurze Produktgeschichte.
Die ersten Windeln waren die Stoffwindeln. Dann wurden die Papierwindeln erfunden.

Auf diesem Fortschritt ruhte sich die ganze Windelindustrie jahrzehntelang aus. Bis man in Amerika die Höschenwindel erfand:

Stellen Sie sich vor, Pampers ist innen eine Windel und außen ein dichtes Plastikhöschen. Zur einmaligen Benutzung.

Durch die Spezialform bietet Pampers dem Baby den besten Komfort. Aber was noch viel wichtiger ist: Pampers hat innen ein einmaliges Trockenvlies, das wie eine Einbahnstraße für Flüssigkeit funktioniert.

Das heißt: Die Flüssigkeit läuft durch das Trockenvlies in eine Saugschicht darunter und kann so gut wie nicht an Babys Haut zurück. Also kann Pampers mit Fug und Recht „mehr Trockenheit" versprechen und „mehr Komfort" als jede herkömmliche Windel.

Wird Pampers' Produktüberlegenheit von den Müttern auch klar erkannt und gewünscht?
In einer Reihe von Produkt-Tests mit den deutschen Müttern wurde Pampers überwältigend bevorzugt – gegenüber allen anderen Windelsystemen. Und zwar gleichbleibend von Test zu Test.

Wir Comptoniken und der Pampers-Erfolg.

Ein kurzer Blick auf den Windelmarkt.
Der deutsche Windelmarkt hatte im Jahre 1972 ein Volumen von stolzen 220 Millionen Mark. Doch mit rund 3 Milliarden Windelwechsel (dominiert durch die Stoffwindel) war dieser Markt noch lange nicht ausgeschöpft.

Angenommen, man gewänne eine größere Zahl Stoffwindel-Benutzer als Höschenwindel-Benutzer, dann wäre ein Marktwachstum in die Richtung von 1 Milliarde Mark sicher möglich.

Mit optimistischen Marktprognosen im Sinn bereiteten wir für Pampers den Testmarkt vor.
Wir wußten, daß wir ein gutes – überlegenes – Produkt hatten. Aber wie der Markt darauf wirklich reagieren würde, konnte uns nur der Markt selbst zeigen. So bereiteten wir mit kalkuliertem Risiko gründlich den Testmarkt vor.

Ausgewählt wurde der Testmarkt Saarland. Aus Gründen der Geheimhaltung möchten wir nicht tiefer ins Detail steigen.

Testmarkt-Werbung –
aber mit welcher Strategie?
Die gesuchte Strategie hatte klar den Vorteil zu definieren, der Pampers – als Innovation – zur Marktführerschaft führen sollte. Es gab hierbei eine ganze Reihe von Produktvorteilen für die Positionierung von Pampers. Zum Beispiel: Überlegene Annehmlichkeit für die Mutter ... die bessere Paßform ... der Komfort für das Baby ...

Aber solchen Vorteilen fehlte einfach das wesentliche Kriterium für eine große, lebensfähige Werbekampagne. Nämlich das Angebot: „Das Baby trocken zu halten", was Ziel und Zweck des Wickelns ist.

Doch gerade Babies trockener zu halten, das kann Pampers auf überlegene Art. So machten wir zum Zentral-Versprechen unserer Testmarkt-Werbung:

„Pampers hilft Ihr Baby trocken halten".
Dieses Versprechen wurde demonstrativ begründet mit dem „Trockenvlies", das die Nässe weg von Babys Haut hält.

Der Stil der Testmarkt-Werbung.
In der Gestaltungs-Strategie hatten wir festgelegt, daß der Trockenvorteil auf eine dramatische, wettbewerbsorientierte Art und Weise herauszustellen sei. Das schaffen wir durch den Systemvergleich der Windeln. Gleichzeitig wollten wir diese Fakten emotionell stark in Baby-Atmosphäre verpacken. Das schaffen wir – besonders in der Fernseh- und Funkwerbung – durch die Autorität der Pampers-Benutzer.

Und wie war der Erfolg?
Nach knapp 8 Monaten Testmarkt wurde Pampers national eingeführt. Mit derselben Werbung wie im Testmarkt.

7a-b

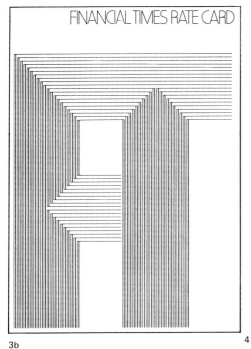

3b

4

6a-c   8   9

Tagebuch aus Mitteltal

1a-b

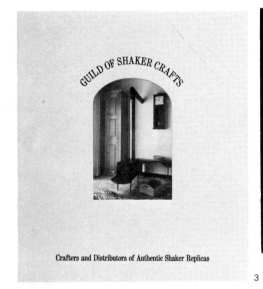

GUILD OF SHAKER CRAFTS

Crafters and Distributors of Authentic Shaker Replicas

3

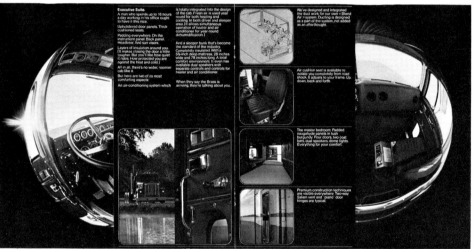

4

6

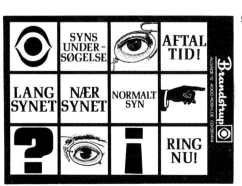

9a-b

10

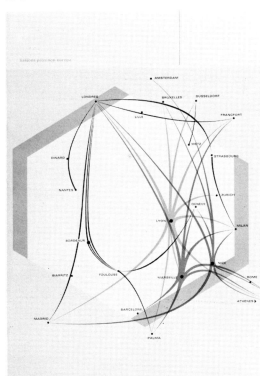

2a-b

5a-b

7

8

1a-b Germany
AD Kurhotel Mitteltal
AG Liebmann & Königsdorf
DIR Bernd Kreutz
PHOTO Jürgen Dommnich
ILL Gerhard Binanzer
COPY Jutta Lücken
Hotel

2a-b United States
AD Dividend Industries Inc.
AG Gauger Sparks Silva
DIR/DES David Gauger
COPY Larry Silva
Housing development, Développement
du logement, Wohnungsbau

3 United States
AD Guild of Shaker Crafts
DES Susan Jackson Keig
Museum replica of Shaker furniture

4 United States
AD International Trucks
AG BBDM Inc.
DIR/DES John Dolby
PHOTO John Dolby
ILL Bob Hunzinger
COPY David Bender
Trucks, Camions, Lastwagen

5a-b France
AD Air France
DIR R. C. Garamond
DES Jacques Nathan-Garamond
Annual report, Rapport annuel,
Jahresbericht

6 France
AD Coignet
AG Primart
DIR/DES Ulrich Meyer
ILL Denise Bourbonnais
Greeting card, Cartes de vœux,
Wunschkarte

7 Germany
AD Pressestelle der Landesregierung
Baden-Württemberg
AG Werbeagentur Günter Bläse
DIR Herr Walter
DES Bruno Haag
ILL Kai Mahrholz

8 Spain
AD Laboratorios Vinas
AG Estudio Moradell
DIR/DES Arcadi Moradell

9a-b Denmark
AD Brandstrup
DIR/DES Erik Alsing
Optician's visiting card, Carte de visite
d'un opticien, Visitenkarte eines
Optikers (a)
Mailing slot (b)

10 Holland
AD Air Taxi Service Rotterdam
AG Bureau PRPS van Hulzen
DIR Joost Tigges
DES Ton Hoogendoorn
Boarding pass, Carte d'embarquement

1

2a-b

4

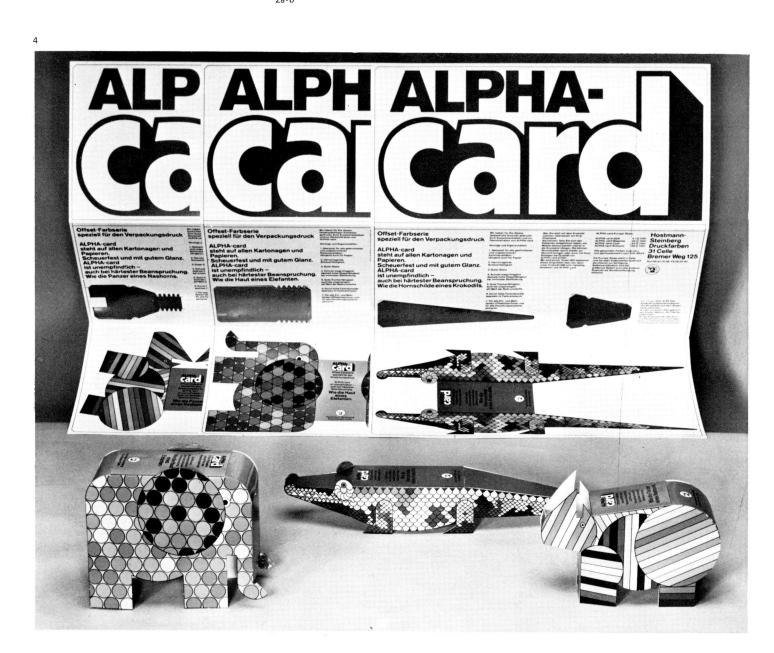

3a-b

5a-b

6a-b

1a-b

1d-e

3

4a-b

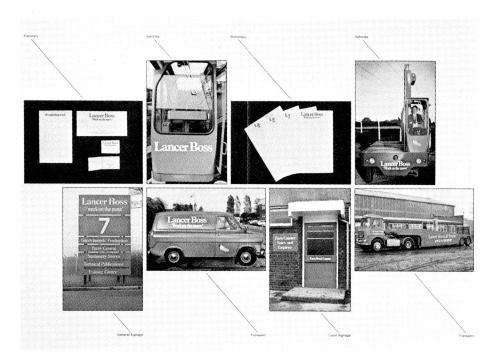

1c

2a-c

1a-f United States
AD NBC Television Network
AG NBC Television Network
Marketing Dept.
DIR Bob Greenwell
DES Ner Beck (a, b, d, e, f)
    Ner Beck and Bob Greenwell (c)
PHOTO Malcolm Emmons and Sport
Magazine (d, e)
COPY Hal Alterman (a, b, d, e)
    Don Eddy (c)
Television programme promotion

2a-c Great Britain
AD Friends Design Workshop
DIR/DES Cliff Richards
Studio Promotion

3 Israel
AD Elite
AG A. Ariely Ltd.
DIR/DES David T. Tartakover
ILL M. Astel
Chocolate

4a-b Great Britain
AD Action Research
AG Derek Forsyth Graphics Ltd.
National campaign for crippled children,
Campagne nationale pour l'enfance
handicapée

5a-b Great Britain
AD/AG Negus & Negus
DIR Dick Negus
DES Priscilla Young
Studio Promotion

1f

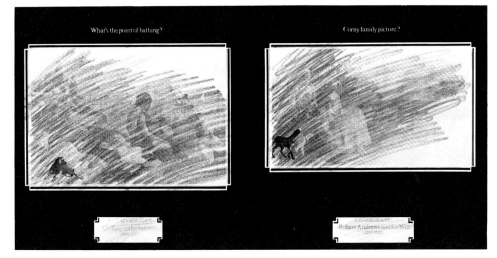

5a-b

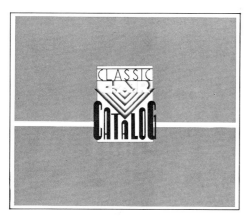
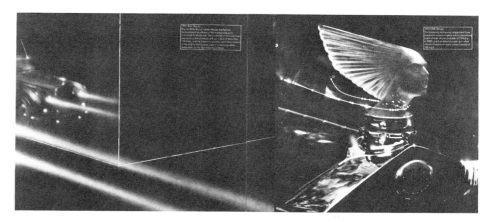

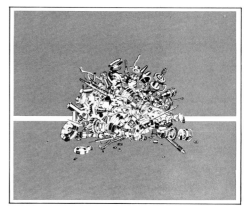

1a-d

3a-d   5   6   7

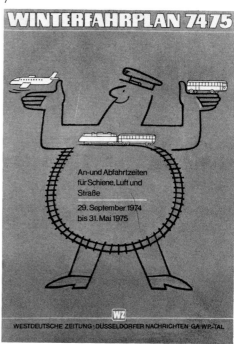

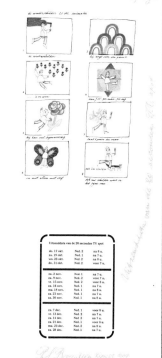

2a-b

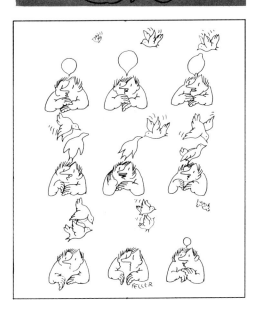

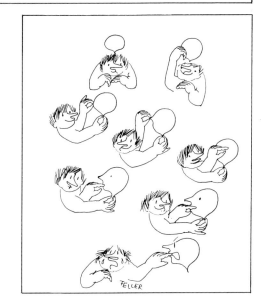

4a-d

1a-d United States
AD Push Pin Graphics
ILL Seymour Chwast, Haruo Miyauchi,
Christine Piper

2a-b Holland
AD Bedrijfschap Schildersbedrijf
AG Nationale Publiciteits
Onderneming BV
DIR/DES Theo Stradman
PHOTO Leo Karr
ILL Max Velthuijs
Housepainting cooperative, Coopérative
de décoration en bâtiment, Maler-
Genossenschaft

3a-d United States
AD Adla
AG The Weller Institute
DIR/DES Don Weller
ILL Glen Iwasaki
Newsletter brochure
Revue

4 Germany
AD V. Jirout
DES Ludvik Feller
Self promotion, Promotion individuelle

5 Germany
AD Haindl Papier GmbH
AG Werbeagentur Peter Seidler
DIR Andreas Asam
DES Bernhard Höhne
ILL Thomas Lüttge
COPY Peter Seidler, Andreas Asam
Paper, Papier

6 Denmark
AD High Fidelity
DES Søren Balle
Hi-Fi

7 Germany
AD Düsseldorfer Nachrichten
DIR H. Desgranges
DES Ludwig Koob
Timetable, Horaire, Fahrplan-Beilage

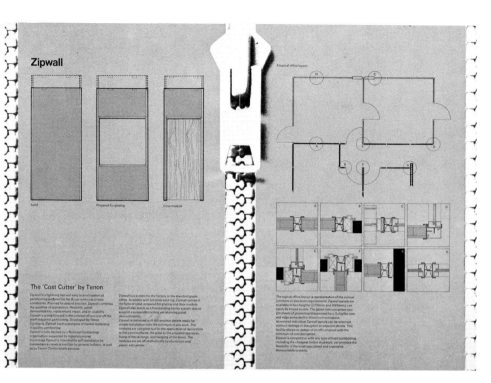

1a–b

4a–b

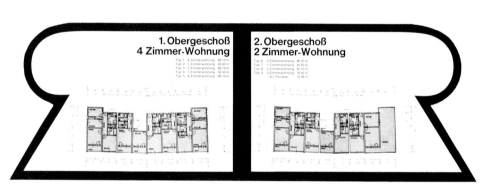

6

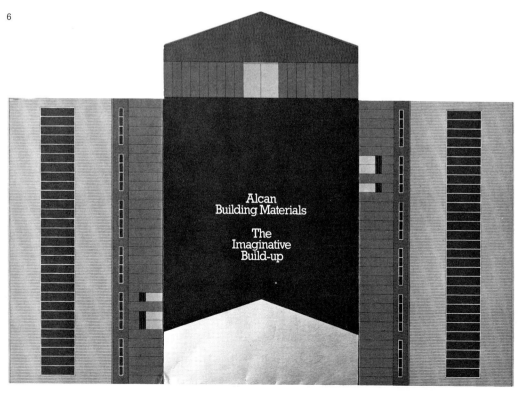
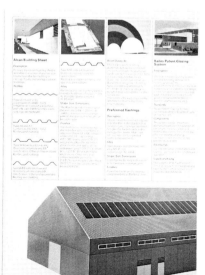

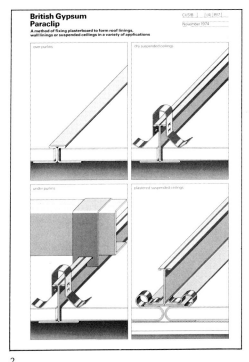

2

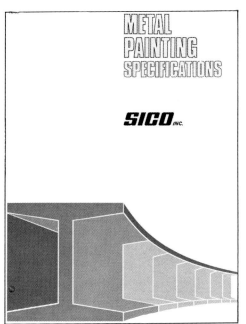

3

5a-b

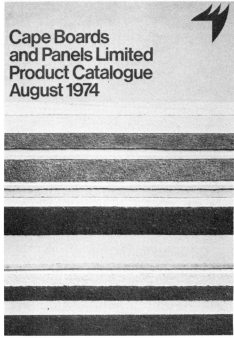

7

1a-b Great Britain
AD Tenon Contracts
AG John Nash & Friends
DIR John Nash
DES Malcolm Smith
A cheap fast partitioning system, Un
système de cloison bon marché et
rapide, Ein billiges und einfaches
System der Raumteilung

2 Great Britain
AD British Gypsum
AG Cope Design Associates
DIR/DES Peter Cope
ILL Christopher Marshall
Suspended ceiling fixing systems,
Systèmes pour suspendre de
faux-plafonds, System zur Fixierung
von hängenden Innenabdeckungen

3 Canada
AD Sico Inc.
AG Zoam
DIR/DES Robert Lennini
Paint specifications, Descriptions de
peintures, Farbenspezifizierung

4a-b Austria
AD HR Schertler Bau Gesellschaft
AG Atelier Wiener
DES Erich M. Wiener
Housing, Logement, Wohnungen
Offset

5a-b Great Britain
AD Cape Boards & Panels Ltd.
AG Pentagram Design Partnership
DIR Colin Forbes
DES Jean Robert
Marinite TRADA Fire-check Leaflet,
Pamphlet sur le contrôle d'incendie,
Feuerbekämpfungsbroschüre

6 Great Britain
AD Alcan Building Materials
AG John Nash & Friends
DIR/DES John Nash
ILL Malcolm Smith
Mailer announcing new company,
Mailer annonçant la naissance d'une
nouvelle compagnie, Postversand-
reklame für eine neue Firma

7 Great Britain
AD Face Delittle
AG Pentagram Design Partnership
DIR/DES John McConnell
Filmsetting house's promotion of new
range of wood letters to be reproduced
for photosetting, Promotion d'une
nouvelle série de lettres de bois,
Reklame für eine neue Kollektion von
hölzernen Buchstaben für Photosätz

1

2

3

6a-b

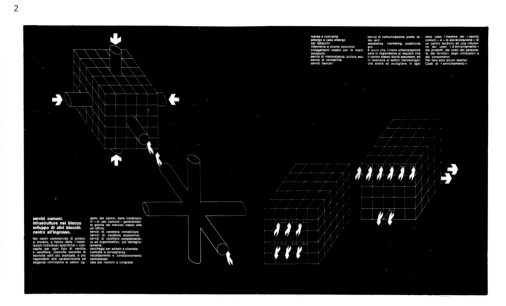

SOFICO

9a-b

Odour and Taste

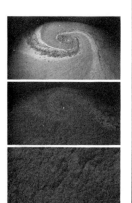

Hand-seasoned industrial products?

Spices may be used dry, grated, or powdered – according to the housewife. The modern food industry has higher requirements in this respect. They demand sterile seasonings, to ensure that their product can be kept longer without spoiling. For this reason natural spices are freed from their germ-infested inactive components, such as cellulose. The practically sterile extracts so obtained are blended into compositions and, according to their intended use, combined with an appropriate carrier, such for example as salt, dextrose, vinegar or oil. Constant intensity of seasoning and constant flavour are the prerequisites for the success of a branded foodstuff.

DER
SIEBDRUCK
1/75

C 21222 E
JANUAR 1975

4

Zeitschrift für Gestaltung 67-III-1974   F 2887 F

form

5

7

8

Strategies
for School
Improvement

10

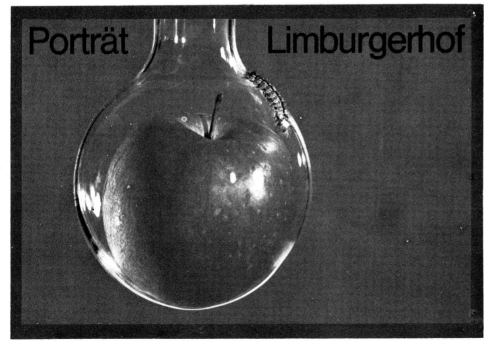

Porträt   Limburgerhof

1 United States
AD Euromoney Publication Ltd.
DES John Constable
Financial journal

2 Poland
AD Concert Music Association
DES J. Rafal Olbinski
Polish concert music fair, Festival de
musique polonaise de concert,
Veranstaltung polischer Konzertmusik

3 Japan
AD/AG Taisho Pharmaceutical Co.
DES Yutaka Sugita

4 Japan
AD Semba Store Group
AG Bolt & Nuts Studio
DES Kenzo Nakagawa
ILL Hiro Nobuyama
Department store, Grand magasin,
Warenhaus

5 Australia
AD Broken Hill Proprietary Company
Ltd.
AG Cato Hibberd Hawksby Pty. Ltd.
ILL Barrie Tucker
Journal for company shareholders,
Revue pour les actionnaires d'une
société, Zeitschrift Aktionäre zur
Aktionäre

6 Great Britain
AD Property Services Agency
AG HMSO Graphic Design
DIR G. Hammond
DES G. Hammond, P. Heatherington
New Government scheme for
co-ordinating interior design colours
for fabrics, paints, etc., Nouveau projet
du gouvernement pour coordonner les
couleurs de tissus d'ameublement et
de peintures intérieures, Neues
Regierungsprogramme für die Koordina-
tion von Farben, Stoffen, usw. für
Innendekoration

7a-b Great Britain
AD Institute of Geological Sciences
AG HMSO Graphic Design
DIR/DES Philip Marriage
ILL Gary Hincks
COPY Susanna van Rose, Ian Mercer
'The story of the Earth', an exhibition in
the Geological Museum, 'L'histoire de
la terre', 'Die Geschichte unserer Erde'

8a-b Germany
AD Bayerischer Rundfunk
DES Walter Tafelmaier
ILL Michael Tafelmaier
Music programmes

9 Great Britain
AD Royal Northern College of Music
AG Royle/Murgatroyd Design
Associates Ltd.
DIR/DES Keith Murgatroyd
Music programmes

10a-b Spain
AD Joventuts Musicals
AG Soley Studio
DIR/DES Santiago Soley
Concert in memory of Pablo Casals,
Concert donné à la mémoire de Pablo
Casals, Konzert im Andenken von Pablo
Casals

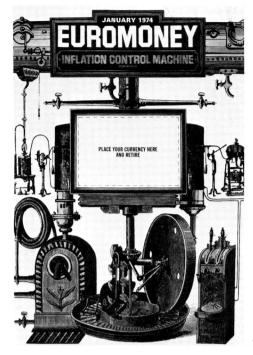

1

2

6

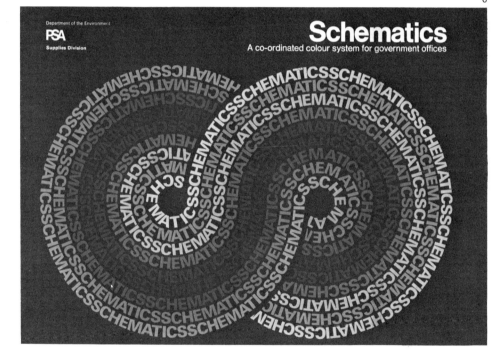

8a-b

Bayerischer Rundfunk Sommerprogramm 1974

3

4

5

7a-b

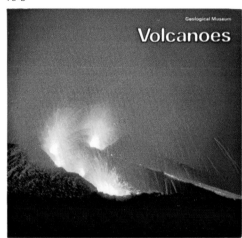

9

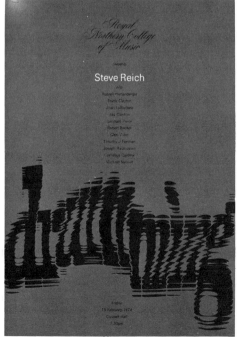

10a-b

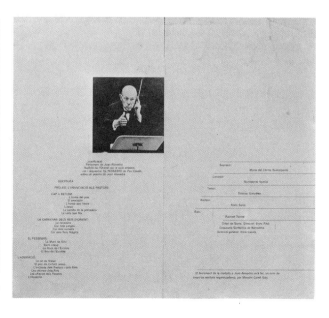

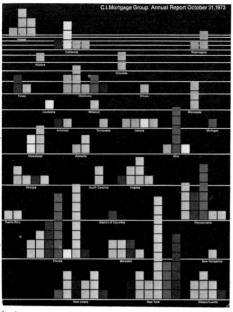

1a-b

rates), rather than on a once-a-month, month-end basis. Further, the practice of structuring loans with interest rate ceilings should diminish in the future. During 1973, a number of such floating loans reached their interest ceiling maximums and as the prime rate continued to rise, their profitability declined. These changes should substantially improve the REIT industry's ability to maintain a predictable lending spread and, hence, profitability during any future periods of abnormal monetary conditions.

Recently, the prime rate has fallen from its peak of 10 percent and monetary forecasts indicate further reductions in this and other short-term interest rates during 1974. During periods of falling interest rates, commercial paper rates normally decline more rapidly than the prime rate and this situation would effect a widening of trust lending spreads from which C.I.Mortgage Group hopes to benefit in 1974.

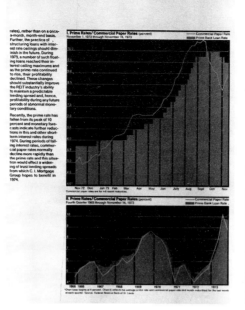

"Medicines should be good formulas, fairly priced and truthfully advertised as, for that matter, should be all other commodities advertised to the public. This company favors any legislation which honestly attempts to accomplish that purpose." From our company's 1933 annual report

2

5a-b

7a-b

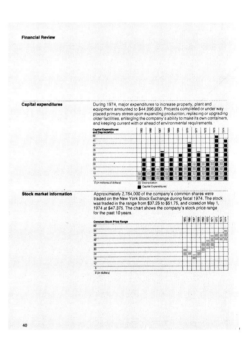

Financial Review

Capital expenditures During 1974, major expenditures to increase property, plant and equipment amounted to $44,096,000. Projects completed or under way placed primary stress upon expanding production, replacing or upgrading older facilities, enlarging the company's ability to make its own containers, and keeping current with or ahead of environmental requirements.

Stock market information Approximately 2,784,000 of the company's common shares were traded on the New York Stock Exchange during fiscal 1974. The stock was traded in the range from $37.25 to $51.75, and closed on May 1, 1974 at $47.375. The chart shows the company's stock price range for the past 10 years.

40

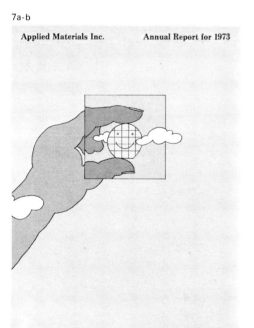

Applied Materials Inc.   Annual Report for 1973

So, to optimize the efficiency of our reactors, we designed and built many of our own components, including precision metering valves, automatic flow controllers and process control programmers. Then, something exciting began to happen.

As we started installing our own components in our systems, people in other industries discovered we were building the kind of precision components they were looking for and—just like that—some nice new markets in the analytical instrumentation and chemical processing industries began to develop.

A couple of decisions are made. Since some of our CVD-related products had applications in non-semiconductor industries, we decided to formally venture, on a controlled basis, into new markets in other industries.

We also decided to expand and diversify our product and customer service base *within* the semiconductor industry to further enhance our position.

And during the past year, our marketing staff was bolstered in all offices and product areas to meet the demands created by these new product/application decisions.

Killing two birds with one stone. Our development staff recently pulled off a rather nice technological coup by coming up with a new product which has immediate application both within the semiconductor industry as well as within a number of other non-semiconductor industries.

The product is called the IN SOURCE ™1500.

10

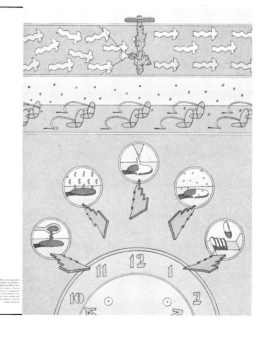

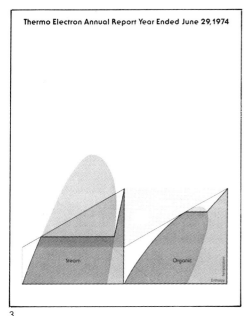

Thermo Electron Annual Report Year Ended June 29,1974

3

Imasco Limited Annual Report 1973

4

6a-c

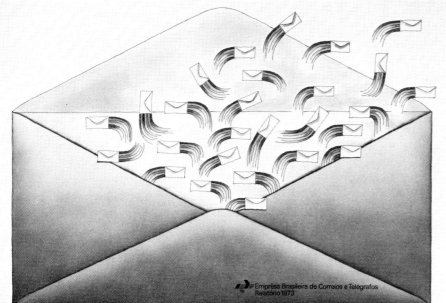

Empresa Brasileira de Correios e Telégrafos
Relatório 1973

1a-b United States
AD C.I. Mortgage Group
AG Corporate Annual Reports
DIR/DES Alicia Landon
ILL Werner Munkenhirn

2 United States
AD Richardson & Merrell Inc.
AG Corporate Annual Reports
DIR/DES Leslie A. Segal
ILL Burt Glinn

3 United States
AD Thermo Electron Corp.
AG Corporate Annual Reports
DIR/DES Len Fury
PHOTO Barbara Fiffer
ILL Jack Doyle

4 Canada
AD Imasco Ltd.
AG Design Collaborative
DIR/DES Ernst Roch
Annual report

5a-b United States
AD H. J. Heinz Co.
AG Harrison Associates
DIR Peter Harrison
DES Jay Tribich
PHOTO Bruce Davidson
Annual report

6a-c Brazil
AD Service Postale
AG A Casa do Desenho
DIR/DES Gian Calvi
COPY Groener
Annual report

7a-b United States
AD Applied Materials Inc.
AG Dennis S. Juett & Associates Inc.
DIR/DES Dennis S. Juett
PHOTO Ron Turner
ILL Dave Bhang
COPY Tom Broener
Annual report

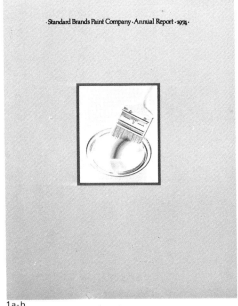

A great deal of our consumer preference information comes from our retail sales personnel. In order to facilitate this flow of information, regular in-store meetings between company executives and salespeople are scheduled throughout the year to provide opportunities for direct comments on new products, serviceability of our existing products and on any customer-oriented problems. These meetings keep the lines of communication open and decrease the company's reaction time to possible changes in local conditions.

The average retail center stocks over 9700 items, all of which are sold at prices which are generally below the prevailing market. Not only are these items stocked in quantities that are normally large enough to satisfy virtually all customer needs, but, in addition, every effort is made to insure completeness of product lines in terms of color selection, pattern selection, and price category.

Many of our products and almost all of our paints are packaged under company labels which, due to extensive advertising and customer satisfaction, are amongst the best known in our trading area.

Paint accounts for 41% of our total sales with the balance as follows: Floorcoverings, 16%; Wallcoverings, 10%; Imports, 9%; Art and Hobby Supplies, 7%; Brushes and Rollers, 6%; and all other products, such as adhesives, ladders and tools, 11%.

For the most part our customers are amateurs who use our products for their own projects. They range from the homeowner re-doing his entire home to the teenager repaint-ing his car; from farmers to vacation vehicle owners; from hobbyists to apartment dwellers. As home maintenance costs continue to soar and overall leisure time increases, more and more people are encouraged toward Do-It-Yourself projects.

These new customers demand larger selections, more and better sales services, qualified sales personnel, exceptional quality and reasonable prices. These are services that have always been provided by Standard Brands Paint Company, and as the needs of our customers are met they become our most enthusiastic supporters, returning again and again and delivering by word of mouth the Standard Brands Paint Company story to their friends and neighbors.

Our manufacturing division, Major Paint and Varnish Company, is one of the industry's most efficient producers of paint and paint products. This Division is responsible for the manufacture of approximately 80% of the paint products currently being marketed through our retail paint and decorating centers. The primary advantage in manufacturing our own products is derived from the control we are able to exert on costs, but of equal importance is the ability to insure adequate shipments of paint and paint products to our stores, maintain rigid quality control, and develop new products to keep abreast of the rapid technological advances in the industry.

During this past year, Major Paint concentrated its efforts on an overall tightening of operating procedures. A conversion to a two-shift basis, plus the further automation of manufacturing processes, has helped stem the upward spiral of general operating costs. Also during the year, Shiva, Inc.'s manufacturing facilities in Paducah, Kentucky were moved to Torrance, California and their production was placed under the supervision of Major Paint and Varnish Company. This move was made primarily to afford us a greater amount of direct control over Shiva's operations.

The construction of our new warehouse, which is scheduled for completion in early 1975, will allow for the addition of 57,000 square feet of manufacturing space to Major Paint's existing 112,640 square feet. This space will be utilized to enlarge our paint production capacity and will house some of the most sophisticated manufacturing and packaging equipment available. In addition, a new color computer that was installed this year will enable us to begin a pilot program of automatically dispensing tinting colorant into batches of paint, thereby eliminating a great deal of manual tinting and color matching. These and other improvements will help us offset the rising costs of raw materials and labor in the year to come.

In fiscal 1974, Major Paint produced 7,378,700 gallons of paint and products allied to the paint industry. The aerosol plant filled 1,925,800 units and the artist colors division produced 1,649,700 tubes.

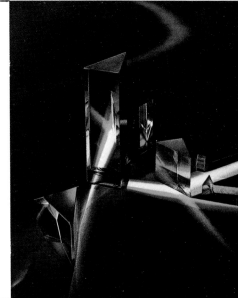

1a-b

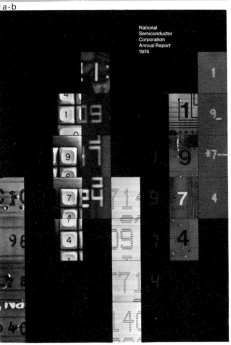

National Semiconductor Corporation Annual Report 1974

3a-c

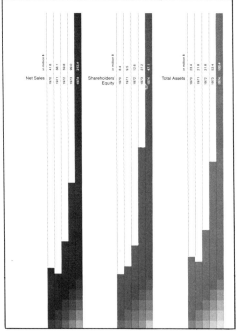

Net Sales in million $					Shareholders' Equity in million $					Total Assets in million $				
1970	41.8				1970	8.4				1970	23.4			
1971	38.1				1971	9.5				1971	21.8			
1972	59.8				1972	12.6				1972	31.8			
1973	99.0				1973	27.2				1973	52.4			
1974	212.8				1974	47.1				1974	100.4			

5a-c

Industry sources estimate that calendar 1974 will be the cross-over point from core to semiconductor memory systems. In terms of dollar sales, Semiconductor memory sales are expected to top a half billion dollars by 1977 and reach a billion in 1980.

New Markets – Microprocessors and memory systems were two of the major market areas penetrated by National during the past year. The IMP (Integrated Micro Processor) family was greatly expanded in both hardware and software.

Your ears deserve
the finest. Give them
the reserved seat
of your choice
by subscribing today.

2a-d

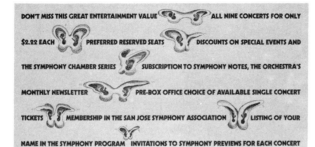

4a-b

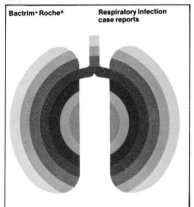

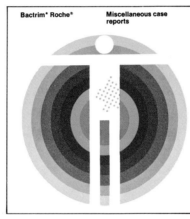

6a-b

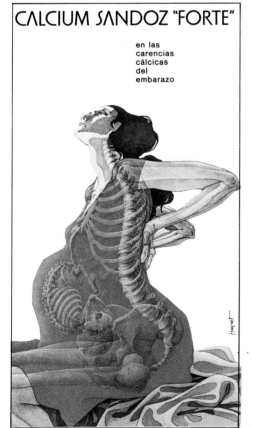

CALCIUM SANDOZ "FORTE"

en las
carencias
cálcicas
del
embarazo

CALCIUM SANDOZ "FORTE"

en las
desmineralizaciones
óseas
del niño

1a-b United States
AD Standard Brands Paint Company
AG The Weller Institute
DIR Don Weller
DES Don Weller, Chikako Matsubayashi
PHOTO Roger Marshutz
ILL Richard Hubner
COPY Sheldon Weinstein
Annual report

2a-d United States
AD San Jose Symphony
AG Sam Smidt & Ass.
DES/COPY Sam Smidt
ILL Kay Wong
Symphony

3a-c United States
AD National Semiconductor Corporation
AG Ken Parkhurst & Ass.
DES Ken Parkhurst
PHOTO Cary Krueger
Annual report

4a-b Canada
AD Hoffmann-La Roche Ltd.
AG Design Collaborative
DIR Rolf Harder, John Malough
DES Rolf Harder
Pharmaceuticals, Medikamente

5a-c United States
AD/AG Smith Kline & French
Laboratories
DIR Alan J. Klawans
DES Kramer, Miller Lomden, Glassman
PHOTO Robert Rich
COPY Len Aulenbach
Pharmaceuticals used in psychiatry,
Medikamente für die Psychiatrie

6a-b Spain
AD Sandoz S.A.E.
AG/DES Enric Huguet
Pharmaceuticals, Medikamente
Offset

Rückblickend auf die vergangenen 25 Jahre

darf man sagen, daß alle, die das Anliegen der Deutschen Wohlfahrts-Briefmarken gefördert haben – und dabei soll auch der anonymste Helfer nicht vergessen sein – guten Grund haben, sich über den Erfolg zu freuen.

Motivreihe: Welt des Spiels
Ausgabe: 1973/74

Weihnachtsmarken

Ab 1969 kamen zu den jetzt 8 Wohlfahrts-Briefmarken einer Serie noch jeweils 2 Wohlfahrts-Weihnachtsmarken hinzu; eine für die Bundesrepublik und eine für Berlin.

Von 1966 an gerechnet, konnte ein durchschnittlicher Jahreserlös aus den Wohlfahrts-Briefmarken von 11,7 Millionen DM

erzielt werden, der von den sechs Freien Wohlfahrtsverbänden verwaltet und zur Hilfe für Kinder und alte Menschen, Kranke und Behinderte verwendet wird. Auch als die Wohlfahrts-Briefmarken nicht mehr in die Sendung der „Aktion Sorgenkind" einbezogen waren, konnte dieser Jahreserlös in etwa gehalten werden, denn als Ausgleich

wurden vom ZDF jeweils sechs Werbespots über die Wohlfahrts-Briefmarken gesendet.

Bei Abschluß der Serie 1973/74 betrug der Gesamterlös aus den 24 bisher erschienenen Serien 136 Millionen DM. Das Verhältnis zwischen Direktvertrieb durch die Post und Verkauf von Seiten der Wohlfahrtsverbände hat sich im Verlauf der Jahre auf 50:50 eingependelt.

Motivreihe: Welt des Spiels
Ausgabe: 1968/69

Motivreihe: Welt des Spiels
Ausgabe: 1969/70

Motivreihe: Märchen-Serie
Ausgabe: 1965/66

Motivreihe: Märchen-Serie
Ausgabe: 1964/65

Die Geschichte der Wohlfahrts-Briefmarken

1a-d

4a-b

The Census Bureau reports that by 1980, university enrollments may have increased by fifty-five percent over 1970.
Because of our fervent wish to be ready, particularly in those areas which will be our concern, to fully offer the University's student and his society, the University must now work toward the completion of the Fine Arts Plaza; we must add facilities for Art, Dance and Music to the recently constructed Laura V. Shaw Theatre and James W. Miller Auditorium.

A task such as this cannot be accomplished by the University alone; we shall need the support of alumni and parents, legislators and friends, corporations and foundations — all agencies and persons who believe in the arts and who hold that they are essential to this nation and its quality of life.
We believe it, and hence the students, faculty, and administrators of Western Michigan University's College of Fine Arts pledge total commitment to the fulfillment of this project.

Robert Holmes, Dean
College of Fine Arts
Western Michigan University
January 1, 1973

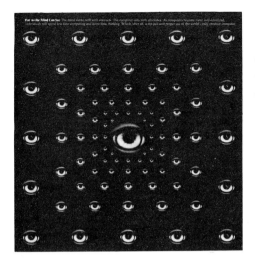

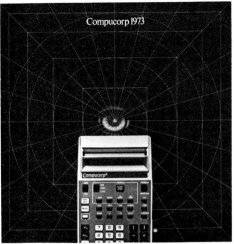

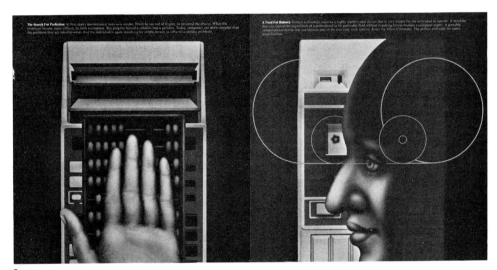

2a-c

3

1a-d Germany
AD BAG – Bundesarbeitsgemeinschaft
der Freien Wohlfahrtspflege, Bonn
AG Werbeagentur Peter Lorenz GmbH
Help given to German welfare
organizations through surplus money of
stamps, Aide donnée aux sociétés de
bienfaisance allemande grâce à
l'excédent de la vente de timbres,
Finanzielle Hilfe für die deutschen
Wohlfahrts-organisationen vom
überschüssigen Postmarkeneinkommen

2a-c United States
AD Compucorp
AD Dennis S. Juett & Associates Inc.
DIR/DES Dennis S. Juett
PHOTO Lamb and Hall
ILL Bill Imhoff
COPY Mel Newhoff
Annual report

3 South Africa
AD Mer-National Laboratories
AG Jeremy Sampson Associates
(Pty.) Ltd.
DIR/DES Jeremy Sampson
PHOTO Alan Keartland
Pharmaceuticals, Medikamente

4a-b United States
AD College of Fine Arts, Western
Michigan University
AG Design Center, Department of Art
DIR/DES Jon Henderson
PHOTO John Carney

5 Great Britain
AD/AG Geigy Pharmaceuticals (UK)
DIR Brian Stones
DES Arthur Samuel
COPY Geoff Downing
Pharmaceuticals, Medikamente

5

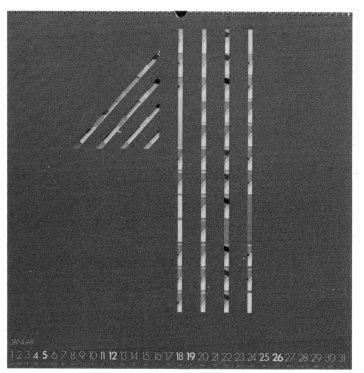

1a-e

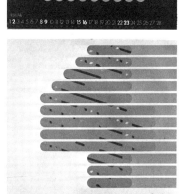

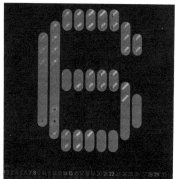

3a-b

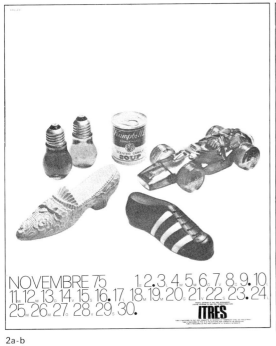

NOVEMBRE 75 1.2.3.4.5.6.7.8.9.10.11.12.13.14.15.16.17.18.19.20.21.22.23.24.25.26.27.28.29.30.

ITRES

2a-b

L'INSOLITO 75

ITRES

Greetings cards,
calendars
Cartes de voeux,
calendriers
Glückwunschkarten,
Kalender

1a-e Germany
AD Domberger Siebdruck
AG Gebhardt und Lorenz
DIR Michael Domberger, Dieter
Gebhardt, Peter Lorenz
DES Gebhardt und Lorenz
COPY Domberger Siebdruck

2a-b Italy
AD Itres S.p.A.
AG Studioelle
DIR Ennio Lucini
DES Giampietro Ceretti
ILL Renzo Bazzani
COPY Ennio Lucini
Calendar

3a-b Germany
AD Zanders
AG Olaf Leu Design
PHOTO Oskar Reiner

4 Germany
AD Roland Offsetmaschinenfabrik
Faber & Schleicher AG
AG Olaf Leu Design
DIR Olaf Leu
DES Olaf Leu, Fritz Hofrichter
Offset machines

4

JULI JULI JULIO JUILLET   AUGUST AUGUST AOÛT AGOSTO

ROLAND OFFSET

1

2

4a-b

PHILIPS introduced a projection television receiver in 1937. As early as 1927 the parent company in Eindhoven built and tested a crystal controlled short wave transmitter operating on 30.92 metres, using their own water cooled valves. Reception extended as far as the East Indies, some 10,000 miles away. Later that year Philips co-operated in relaying the first BBC Empire Broadcast.

Models: Carole Singleton, Paul North. Airfield: La Ferte Alais.

3a

3b

Greetings cards, calendars
Cartes de voeux, calendriers
Glückwunschkarten, Kalender

1 United States
AD James Marchael
AG The Design Partnership
DIR Jack Weiss
DES Les Holloway
ILL/COPY James Marchael
Calendar, Calendrier

2 Holland
AD 4P Drukkerij Reclame BV
AG Loridan BV
PHOTO Frans Voss, Theo Uijtenhaak

3a-b United States
AD/AG Push Pin Studio
ILL Seymour Chwast (a)
 Haruo Miyauchi (b)
Calendar, Calendrier

4a-b Great Britain
AD Philips Electrical Ltd. (U.K.)
AG Wasey Campbell-Ewald Ltd.
DIR/DES Arnold Schwartzman
PHOTO Sarah Moon
COPY Tony Peverett
Calendar for 50th anniversary of Philips
Electrical, Calendrier pour le 50ème
anniversaire de P.E.

5 Germany
AD Volkswagenwerk AG
AG Alpha 9 photo-team
DIR/DES Albrecht Cropp
Automobiles

6 Brazil
AD/AG Gian Calvi
Greetings card, Carte de vœux

5

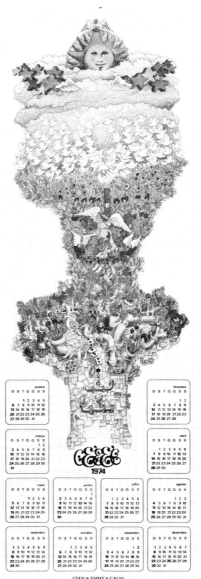

GIAN & EMMY & CALVI
Criação em Artes Gráficas

6

1a-b

4a-b

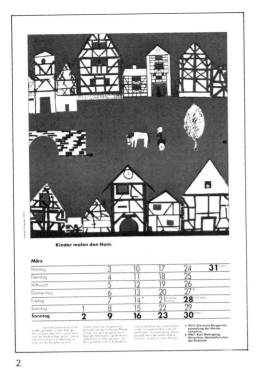

Kinder malen den Hain.

März

Montag		3	10	17	24	31
Dienstag		4	11	18	25
Mittwoch		5	12	19	26
Donnerstag		6	13	20	27
Freitag		7	14	21	28
Samstag	1	8	15	22	29
Sonntag	**2**	**9**	**16**	**23**	**30**

2

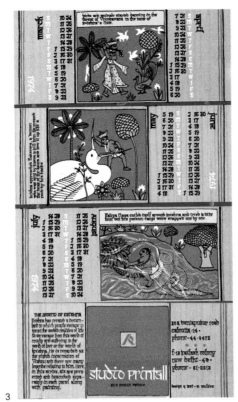

3

5

6

7a-b

Greetings cards,
calendars
Cartes de voeux,
calendriers
Glückwunschkarten,
Kalender

1a-b Spain
AD Industrias Graficas Casamajo
DIR/DES Tomas Vellve
ILL Jaime & Jorge Blassi

2 Germany
AD Hainer Initiative
DIR/DES Wolfgang Schmidt
Conservation and revitalization,
Conservation et renaissance,
Konservation

3 India
AD Studio Printall
DES M. Mullick

4 Great Britain
AD Asahi Pentax Ltd.
DIR Sam Haskins
DES M. Katsui
PHOTO Sam Haskins

5 Great Britain
AD/AG International Graphic Press Ltd.

6 Brazil
AD Esso Brasileira de Petro
AG McCann Erickson
DIR/DES Vítor Lemos
ILL Oliveira Monte
COPY Gustavo Waennheldt

7a-b Switzerland
AD Handelsgenossenschaft des
Schweiz. Baumeisterverbandes
AG Gisler & Gisler
DIR/DES Jacques Lehnen
PHOTO Marcel Hayoz
Master builders, Entrepreneurs de
bâtiments, Baumeister

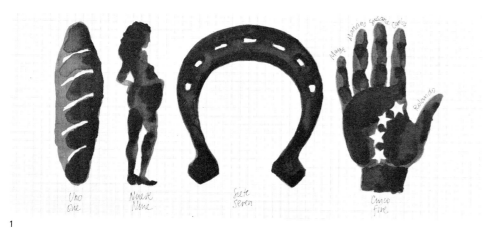

1

2

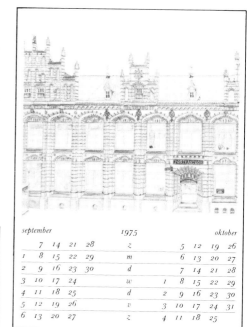

3

6a-d

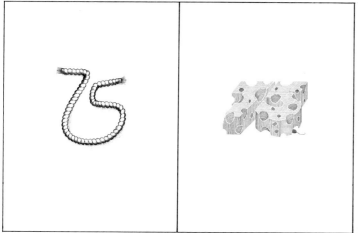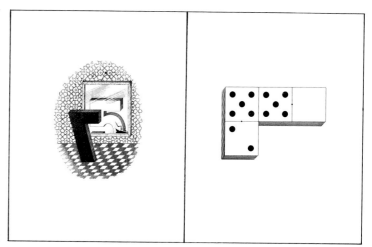

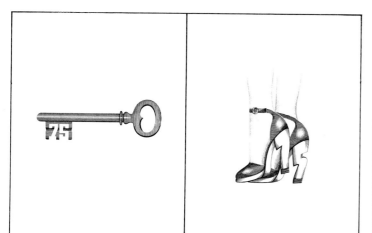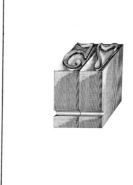

Wir verloben uns
Ursula Preiß
Joachim Manke

1. Juni 1974
Lohr (Main)

4

5

Season's Greetings The Hong Kong Trade Development Council

7

8

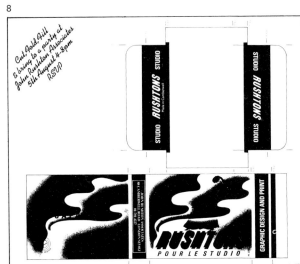

9

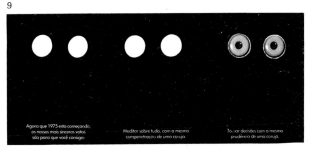

Greetings cards,
calendars
Cartes de voeux,
calendriers
Glückwunschkarten,
Kalender

1 Spain
AD Carlos Rolando & Asociados
DIR/DES Carlos Rolando
Christmas card

2 France
AD/AG Bristol
DIR Delcourt
DES Jean Larcher
Greetings card

3 Holland
AD Centrale Directie der PTT
DES Letty Vos

4 Germany
AD Ursula Preijs
DIR/DES Wilhelm Malkemus
Engagement announcement, Annonce
de fiançailles, Verlobungsanzeige

5 Hong Kong
AD The Hongkong Trade Development
Council
AG Graphic Communication Ltd.
DIR/DES Henry Steiner
Greetings card

6a-d France
AD Jean Larcher
AG Jean Larcher Studio
Greetings card

7 Japan
AD Package Design Studio Forme
DES Kimikiko Arita
Greetings card

8 Great Britain
AD/AG John Rushton Associates
DIR John Rushton
DES Mark Osborne
Party invitation – publicity

9 Brazil
AD Celpa – Centrais Elétricas
do Pará S.A.
AG Mendes Publicidade
DIR/DES A. Alessio

Greetings cards, calendars
Cartes de voeux, calendriers
Glückwunschkarten, Kalender

1 Brazil
AD Creditum
AG Fator Publicidade
DIR Gesse Alves Pereira
Christmas card

2 Great Britain
AD/AG Young & Rubicam Ltd.
DIR Tago Byers
Christmas card

3a-c Great Britain
AD/AG Pentagram Design Partnership
DIR/DES John McConnell
Christmas mailing – matches puzzle
book, Courrier de Noël – livre sur les
casse-têtes à allumettes, Weihnachts-
reklame – Zündholz-Puzzlebuch

4 Holland
AD/DES Pieter Brattinga
Christmas card, Carte de Noël

5 Great Britain
AD Austrian National Tourist Board
DIR/DES Stan Krol
Invitation card, Carte d'invitation

6 Great Britain
AD Genevieve Group of Restaurants
DES Royston Cooper
COPY Joseph Berkman
Christmas card

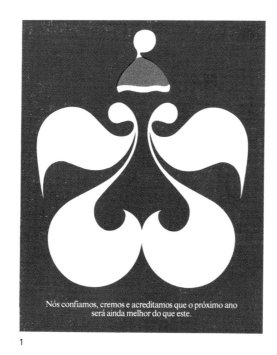

1

2

3a-c

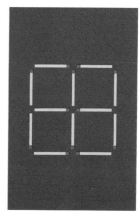

5a-b

4

6

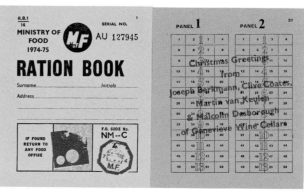

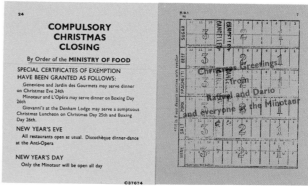